Shedding
and Literally Dreaming

Shedding
and Literally Dreaming

Verena Stefan

Afterword by Tobe Levin

Shedding translated by Johanna Steigleder Moore and
Beth E. Weckmueller
Literally Dreaming translated by Johanna Albert and
Tobe Levin
"Euphoria and Cacophony" translated by Tobe Levin

The Feminist Press
at The City University of New York
New York

Published 1994 by The Feminist Press at The City University of New York,
311 East 94 Street, New York, NY 10128

94 95 96 97 98 5 4 3 2 1

Library of Congress Cataloging-in-Publication Data

Stefan, Verena, 1947–
    [Häutungen. English]
    Shedding and Literally dreaming / Verena Stefan ; afterword by
Tobe Levin ; Shedding translated by Johanna Steigleder Moore and
Beth E. Weckmueller ; Literally dreaming translated by Johanna
Albert and Tobe Levin ; Euphoria and cacophony translated by Tobe
Levin.
    p. cm.
    ISBN 1-55861-081-2 (alk. paper) : $32.50. – ISBN 1-55861-084-7
(pbk. : alk. paper) : $14.95
    1. Stefan, Verena, 1947– –Translations into English.
2. Feminism–Fiction. 3. Women–Fiction. I. Levin, Tobe. II.
Stefan, Verena, 1947– Wortgetreu ich träume. English.
III. Title.
PT2681.T3566Z51513   1994   94-25714
833'.914–dc20   CIP

This publication is made possible, in part, by public funds from the
National Endowment for the Arts and the New York State Council on
the Arts. The Feminist Press is also grateful to Joanne Markell and
Genevieve Vaughan for their generosity.

Cover design by Catherine Hopkins
Text design by Paula Martinac

Typeset by AeroType, Inc., Amherst, New Hampshire
Printed in the United States of America on acid-free paper by McNaughton &
Gunn, Inc., Saline, Michigan

Contents

Shedding

Shadow Skin

I come unexpectedly out of winter into the cascade of greening birches. In Berlin this birch green erupts overnight, yellow-tinged, phosphorescing out of another world. During the usual morning walk to the subway, something appears changed. Not until I am able to relate the onset of numbness back to greening birch trees can I recognize what it is. The first pleasure—the anticipation of perpetual warmth from the sun—lets me breathe freely again and smile. But at second glance the green strikes my eyes like a neon light:

What did I do last year after the first days of birch greening? Was I even alive between April of last year and March of this? I had forgotten that this kind of green existed. I had not forgotten the sun, nor the cold, nor the longing for warmth, but had forgotten that spring brings with it something more than sun, forgotten that there are birch trees that open their floodgates of green.

Each year I find it disconcerting. In other places anemones crocuses daisies already bloom, forsythia as well, but not here on the streets where I live, on these streets the birches are the first to blossom forth overnight. Time, the past, the uncertain future, the year whizzing past—nothing else reminds me of these things as sharply and as painfully. Seven years in Berlin, every year this birch episode. Two, three, years ago the green began to hurt my eyes. I hurry through these interludes. I must try and remember. What else can I hold onto now? This is when my new year begins. In my chronology it is this iridescent green shock that signals that which the calendar shows as New Year's Eve. I am filled with anxiety because I cannot remember the past year.

This birch greening, the energy that flows from it, is no everyday event. I cannot live this way every day—young woman suddenly bursts into flames on the street.

Weeks later and again overnight, when the chestnut trees blossom forth like burgeoning candelabra, I have calmed down a bit. Later still, by the time we can sit beneath the towering chestnut tree and drink a beer without feeling chilly, I will have been swept along by the tide of everyday events; soon the first snowfall will come without my even noticing.

On the way home I pass a tavern. Two men and two women are sitting at a table right next to the sidewalk. Noticing me, one of the men is taken aback. He remarks to the others. They turn to stare at me.

I am wearing a long skirt and a sleeveless T-shirt. In one hand I carry a shopping bag, which holds three bottles of wine. The man leans over the railing and stares fixedly at me as I approach. Something about this situation alarms me more than usual. The man's expression is not lustful or lewd but, instead, quite righteously indignant. As I pass him, he says, incensed: Hey baby, what happened to your boobs?

My spine stiffens. The man is twice my size and half-drunk besides. The others laugh in agreement. Two steps later I hear the shrill catcall whistling past my ears. From the corner of my eye I see the men's legs and hear, after the whistle: Jesus, what knockers!

I crouch, ready to pounce. And then what? I ready myself to lash out. How to attack? Only five more steps until I can push open the heavy door to the building, rest the shopping bag next to the mailbox, take out the mail, go through the inner courtyard to the side entrance, climb the two flights of stairs, unlock the apartment door, enter the kitchen, open the refrigerator, carefully place the three bottles of wine on the shelf, let the door close, and look about the kitchen, arms hanging down at my sides. My breasts hang against my ribcage, warm, sun-filled gourds. Under them tiny rivulets of sweat had gathered and now dissolve, one drop at a time.

It is noon. In eight hours I have a discussion group meeting; how am I to get through the afternoon? My veins stand out, the blood pulsing dark blue. I have to sit down. To be able to strike back just once instead of having to pile up layer upon layer of indignation within myself! What use is the typewriter now? Letters are small dark signs, alien beings that creep about in disarray. I sweep them from the table.

4   *Shedding and Literally Dreaming*

If I proceed from the assumption that it makes sense to do so, I can arrange the letters. I can sit down with them on the floor and select some. I can line them up so that, when other people go through the same process reading them, the letters will yield the sequence:

```
W    H    E                   N
W    I                   L    L
T         H    E    D    A         Y
   C           O         M              E
W    H    E                   N
W         O    M         E              N
```

I pile the letters together again. As if lining them up would bring this day nearer! As if the revolt of women were a matter of one day! It is something composed of bits and pieces, put together one by one.

I line up new letters. Meanwhile, in the tavern the man is smugly finishing his beer. Perhaps he is still talking to the others about my breasts, while I sit on the floor and spell.

Before I started going to school, there was a time when I bathed myself in the kitchen. I was given a basin filled with warm water and then left to myself. In the adjoining room my parents' voices disposed of the events of the day one by one. It was during one of these evening hours that the feeling of actually being alive so overwhelmed me that I was unable to stir. For a few seconds I was intensely aware of every fiber, every pore of the skin that enveloped my body. Then in a flash the tingling pores came together again, bonding together to yield a sensation of completeness which was new to me. This is how it must have been when the first human being was created, I thought. This is exactly how she must have felt! From then on I waited every evening for this sensation of being created, waited every evening to be created anew.

There was the pain. Had it finally happened?

It was already my third attempt at being deflowered. In the meantime I was nearly twenty years old. It couldn't go on like this.

The final tribal ritual is planned and decided alone, carried out in isolation. The only directions handed down, cryptic accounts of pain and blood. I hadn't imagined it would be so complicated.

In some way it all related to my body. It was complicated, too. I dragged around its lifeless parts. It did not measure up to standards. It didn't look youthful. It didn't have a good figure. To me, my body seemed old, my figure outmoded. I hid inside dark shapeless sweaters and skirts. In my dreams I was always "well built," slender, flat-chested, and had no problems fitting into standard sizes.

I knew people who taught me to be aware of my body. I tried to plant the soles of my feet on the ground and to inhale from the top of my head to the tips of my toes, tried to be totally attuned to each present moment in life instead of jumping ahead to the next, tried not to let my thoughts rush through life from one moment to the next but, instead, tried to live here and now.

That was a delaying tactic; it laid the foundation. Although occasionally I got the feeling that I could occupy my whole body, I was nonetheless evicted from it piece by piece. The pride I felt at my first bra, my first girdle, my first lipstick! Initiation rites and models moved in on me from all sides.

The yearning for the man of my dreams had gnawed its way into my very marrow. I was spending a lot of time with Ines in those days; she was different. She wasn't going with anybody; she was going with herself. We touched upon that subject once. We were sitting in her little Citröen after school—she was the first in our class to get her driver's license; it was pouring outside. Ines spoke hesitantly. She was afraid she was not normal, she didn't feel attracted to men. Something was wrong with her, she said. It bothered her. No one used the word *homosexuality*, but a sense of uneasiness lingered.

Ines dared to make the leap. During the summer vacation she took off on her own to hitchhike. We were sixteen or seventeen then. Beforehand we went together to buy her first tampons. Just in case, she said. A feeble attempt at protection against rape.

These pioneer days with Ines were short-lived. Something was lacking when I was with her, despite shared thoughts and experiences. I felt unfulfilled. I fended off her peculiar admiration and encroachment. It was embarrassing. After all, Ines was a woman, how could she give my life any meaning, how could she conquer me?

The first time that I seriously thought about being deflowered, I didn't even get as far as an attempt, although I had made up my mind to do so. Love could not eliminate my fear of it. The feelings that I had collected and stored up waiting for a man were enough to alleviate the problem of sexuality.

The penis protruded from the male body, alien, unlike anything else. It was not so much the fear of becoming pregnant but, rather, that this dangling rank appendage repulsed me. Still, I carefully prepared myself to have intercourse for the first time. I could not remain ignorant forever. Time stood still as I made my way to the doctor's office. The doctor, a woman, gave me a lecture on motherhood and threw me out. In Bern, in 1965, it was still difficult to get the pill. It was a relief to know that, for the time being, life would go on as before.

But the problem remained.

By now it was far from being a question of love. Neither did I believe that I would become more mature by doing it. But men would find me acceptable. An experienced man would be best, I thought. I had read enough to be aware of the importance of empathy and patience. A thirty-year-old acquaintance of mine who occasionally confided in me about his love affairs seemed trustworthy enough to join in the venture.

"No. I won't do that!" he exclaimed, jumping up, shocked. "Of course you'll never forget that first man, you know. You might get too attached. . . ." I didn't understand him. This time I was really determined. A couple of weeks later he agreed after all. "Well, all right," he said, succumbing to the momentary urge to have sex. "I suppose you have to get deflowered sooner or later, and I'd rather be the one to do it than some brutal guy. . . ." He was attracted to very young, boyish girls. "You don't have to take your clothes off," he said, to my relief, as I stood in front of him in my slip and bra. Then he lay on top of me, breathing heavily. He had also cautioned me that I wouldn't be able to "do without" once I had had it. Far away, down in my abdomen, his penis ran up against something that was tightly stretched and would not yield.

I couldn't breathe, couldn't move. I hated having to gasp for air. He tried to run his fingers tenderly through my hair, asked several times whether I was enjoying it. I nodded, knowing he needed reassurance. "You could have moved with me a little bit better," he said when it was over. I couldn't believe my ears. What did he mean? I would have had to invent the motions. Besides, it had all been for nothing. I was not deflowered.

The third time it went on for three nights. After that I stopped bleeding, and it gradually stopped hurting. I was in love. It didn't bother him that I was a virgin. I had to take advantage of this opportunity.

I stood there for a few moments before joining him in bed. The moonlight streaming in through the windows seemed to be a good omen. Should I take *all* my clothes off? Let him worry about that, I decided. Would I measure up to his expectations? Beforehand, in the bathroom, as I ran a comb through my hair one last time and dabbed a few drops of perfume behind my ears, I had shuddered at the thought of my body. Out in public I could smile and draw attention to my slender features, my small hands. But now the issue was hips, breasts, legs. It was impossible to camouflage anything.

For a while we lay side by side, motionless. Where were the other women? The primordial drums were silent. The circle of women had scattered to the four winds, their words at the well had died away, reduced to mere beauty shop gossip (Is your hair naturally curly, or did you get a permanent? No, my natural hair is dull and straight as a board. Yeah, mine too! Now I wish it were straight again). Three hasty kisses had propelled him from my shoulder to my neck to my mouth. The world belonged to me; men would lie at my feet.

"Is it safe today?" he asked.

I hadn't even thought about that. I nodded, counting feverishly. Had I even bothered to make note of my periods these past few months? Never mind—surely nothing would happen the first time.

Cool moistness between my legs. Is that from him or from me? While he sleeps, I slide stealthily to the side, peer at the sheet. The moon, the only thing one can depend on, provides me light. I see dark splotches. It seems to have happened. Yet the pain continues the next night as well. Did it always take so long?

Deeply, breathe deeply all the way down, relax relax, do not hold your breath, breathe rhythmically right down to where the pain is, surely *we* can stand that little bit of pain! said the gynecologist as he did the dilation and curettage after removing my IUD. We certainly can't give you an anesthetic for this kind of thing, whatever gave you that idea! A little D & C, that's nothing!

And in he plunges, cold metal penetrating the mouth of the cervix, one scrape against the cavern walls—five seconds, ten?

How can women stand a whole abortion without anesthetics? I feel sick. Once again I can't breathe. Must I always be gasping for air? The gynecologist leisurely tugs off his gloves, straddles the chair at his desk, and reaches for the dictaphone: "The patient . . ."

The decision to have an IUD inserted had not been mine alone. It was a decision I arrived at while working on "Frauenhandbuch Nr. 1." Up until then I had been on the pill—for four years. The doctor who had finally given me the prescription pointed out that I was a likely candidate for varicose veins. Every so often I used to go off for a while, but basically I kept taking it until one particular evening in Berlin, when Samuel had a visitor. "A really dynamite woman is coming over tonight, a terrific comrade," he said. I felt my insides contract. His pronouncement meant that this was a "comrade" well versed in political expertise; otherwise, he would not have heralded her arrival in such lofty terms. He would most likely have an animated conversation with her; I would sit back and listen. She wanted to talk to Samuel about the pill and the politics of the pharmaceutical industry.

This time, though, I was not merely an onlooker, as was usually the case in conversations between Samuel and his friends and acquaintances. I was amazed at how knowledgeable she was, especially since she was not in the medical profession. Together with other women she was working on a book about abortion and contraception, and she told us about a woman whose uterus had totally shriveled up since she had been taking the pill.

"Actually, I've never really paid any attention to my female organs," I said. "I've never really given the matter much thought. But now that I think about it, I wouldn't really mind if my uterus did shrivel up, then at least I wouldn't have to worry . . ."

Samuel rummaged through his file folders. He seemed to be well informed about the "pill problem" (he was interested in the pharmaceutical industry's profits). How come he hadn't talked to me about this? After all, I was the one who was taking the pill.

A few months later I decided to try out the new Copper T. The idea of varicose veins worried me. Ever since I'd been working at the hospital, I'd been having pains in my legs. Samuel was away on vacation—I didn't really discuss it with him very much. The decision was made with the help of the women from "Bread ♀ Roses," with whom I had recently begun working. On the same day I was supposed to have the IUD put in, the rally by women's groups against section 218* was scheduled to take place in Cologne. The two events had happened to fall on the same day. There was a long wait for an

---

*The federal statute that outlawed abortion in Germany before 1974.

appointment at the clinic, and, because I didn't want to postpone having the IUD put in, I didn't want to cancel mine.

Samuel was furious. He considered me irresponsible for wanting to fly to Cologne right after. I refused to change my mind. Somehow I couldn't help but get the idea that what he really wanted was to keep me from going to the rally.

Having it put in was painless. Afterward, while I was sitting having a quick breakfast with Samuel, I started to get cramps in the pelvic area, just like menstruation. My uterus was contracting.

Samuel drove me to the airport, not saying a word. Close to tears, I finally said that, whenever I really needed someone, I certainly couldn't depend on him. He said that, if I were going to be so unreasonable, he really didn't give a damn what happened to me.

In Cologne the women at the rally took care of me. They wanted to know exactly how it had gone, whether I was in pain. A few hours later the pain subsided, and it didn't bother me at all during the rally.

I could never tell whether the IUD was in the right place. We hadn't found out about self-examination yet. I didn't know where the cervix was, what it looked like, that thing the penis sometimes bumped up against. The vagina—a dark opening. What was behind it? Were there pearls in the depths of this body, coral reefs?

Could a lover's hands bring back to life the lost awareness of one's own body? Wasn't it that which we were seeking during the fleeting hours of a night, the split second of an orgasm / what is an orgasm? To be able to breathe deeply, to once fill every crevice from the shoulder blades to the pelvis, to feel, grow warm, be! To unfurl all the folds of the body, to be free from all tension and rigidity.

To become whole.

Could sexuality be the means through which I could piece together the fragments, restore the oneness from head to foot? If, embracing, I could feel the tautness of all muscles and then afterward savor the release of tension, if, touching another's skin, I could from a distance get in touch with my own, would I then experience sensations that had never surfaced before? Could *I know* another human being? Could I possibly come to know *the nature* of the other's existence?

"You still have quite a way to go," he said. "You didn't have an orgasm."

I froze. How could he presume to know that?

It was the third night we had slept together. It still hurt; there was still blood on the sheet.

"I did," I insisted. "I had one!"

I turn away, cover myself with the protective blanket, and think, What business is it of his?

I would practice and practice, somehow I'd manage to get the hang of it.

> The woman moving with you in coitus
> comes from far away
> look at her closely
> the woman you lie upon!
> behind her gape deserts and abysses.
> she has put long stretches of forgetting
> behind her, fragments of heart strewn in rubble,
> boulders pushed before fresh wounds
> her feelings are worn to the bone.
> years spent on the icy sheet of your fears
> the peaks of emotional poverty rounded so gently
> so velvety so pliant.
> she bears an ocean
> of pent up orgasms inside, which she
> will never in a lifetime be able to pour out
> time is of the essence, thoughts burn, she is
> a cry in the wilderness, the woman
> you lie upon
> look at her closely!
> not this warm body
> beneath you
> is reality
> what you take for reality is only the bat
> of an eye, a pause between
> many realities before and
> after

At eye level shimmered the finely grained heat waves of summer. Finished with high school, I was finally on the road. I started out with Ines, though there was nothing much between us anymore. We had gone our separate ways. The years together with my first man had left their mark. He had become the focal point of my thoughts, at the expense of my imagination. Ines found me boring. We soon parted.

With each step I tried to gain a foothold in the world. I wanted to experience everything, expose myself to everything, let myself be molded. Vulnerable to the point of self-sacrifice, accommodating to the point of destruction, I blindly groped my way southward. The initial fear slowly subsided, but I couldn't shake off a persistent and unmistakable sense of uneasiness. I wasn't at home in the world—I was a guest. I found myself in alien territory. I had sneaked in, unseen; I had dared to proceed on my own—what would happen when men noticed me?

I kept on smiling. With a mysterious smile I asked for asylum in the world, begged for admittance with downcast eyes, with a voice soft and sweetly obsequious. If I stop smiling and glare or strike back at a man who is pestering me, then I am "bitchy," "brazen"—and imperiled.

I am standing at Wittenbergplatz waiting for the traffic light to turn green. In my left hand I am carrying a shopping bag filled with groceries, in my right a jumbo package of toilet paper. I can sense two men approaching me from behind, and I glance back over my shoulder. Just then the man on my left gets hold of a handful of my hair, which is tinted red and shoulder length; he scrutinizes the strands gliding through his fingers and says to his friend: Terrific hair! I whirl around and hit him in the face with the toilet paper, using it as a club to extend my reach. Then, drained of strength, knees shaking, I cross the street. My arm is now heavy as lead; I can no longer lift it. The two men follow me, cursing angrily and calling me names for having had the audacity to stand up to them. On the other side of the street I turn around once more, hiss at them to shut up. They would really like to come after me, but it is broad daylight, and there are people on the street; the two of them are foreigners. Sitting in the subway, I woefully study my small hands. With them alone I could not have landed even one blow. An everyday occurrence. The everyday treatment of a woman, second-class citizen not only in the third world. I probably have a nicer apartment, more social contacts, better working conditions, than most of the foreign workers in West Berlin. But every man—foreign or native—can, regardless of living or working conditions, mistreat me at any time he pleases. Do I have better living conditions simply because I may have a nicer apartment than my oppressor?

At that time I had long hair. I've always been slight; it's always been easy to put an arm around me. It was obvious that I couldn't hitchhike alone—I would have to find another woman if I wanted to come through more or less unscathed. There was no other woman. How could I get to know the world on my own? It was dangerous. To get entangled with a man would mean becoming a participant in his sex life, whatever that might involve. That was just as dangerous. Why couldn't I travel without fear of being molested; why was this direct access to the world closed off to me? At that point I was still inquisitive enough to attempt to experience the world on my own. But later on I realized I could only gain access to the world with the help of middlemen. I made it to Athens without having to have intercourse.

In the youth hostel I finally met up with other women who were traveling alone. A black woman from the United States and a woman from India. But I found no one who wanted to go to northern Europe. Athens in August, waves of heat washing over me. To be able to lose myself in the South, dissolve into a day without end, to end this vacation from the north and begin instead an endless day of perpetual warmth!

This feeling of contentment was short-lived. I was gradually overcome by the fear of not finding anyone with whom I could hitchhike back. It would have been inconceivable for me to go and stand alone beside one of the roads leading out of Athens. Seeing no other way out, I fell in love with a guy who was bumming around the world. With him I traveled all the way across Europe and up to London. I had once spent a few pleasant weeks there with Ines, a summer without entanglements, without fear. This time the city was closed to me.

I felt myself being swept along through London's streets, but the city itself remained inaccessible. I began searching for people who had already gained access. At Piccadilly Circus I attached myself to an easygoing group and went with them to their house. We drank tea, smoked hash, and listened to music. That same evening they left on vacation. I kept edging along the city, constantly losing my sandals.

In the subway—I filled my lungs with the black, tarlike odor, at least that was real—an American commented on the faded blue shirt I was wearing. I smiled, relieved. We made a date for that evening. Changing trains, as he stood on the step shifting his weight from one foot to the other, he suddenly kissed me. I drew back; he chuckled in gleeful anticipation: Only kidding, baby. Watch out for the doors! To spend just one evening in this city with one of them instead of being hassled by all the rest, is that asking too much? I stood there pleading with myself.

"That's hard to believe, a girl on vacation all by herself and not in the mood for it?" one of the men who had given me a ride in Saloniki had said, perturbed. "Are you sure I can't help you out?" I didn't understand why he said that. I didn't want sex. I wanted to see foreign countries.

I had so totally blocked out the expected norms of behavior that I was incapable of realistically judging the actual situation in which I found myself.

The American paid my way into the movie. He bought a bottle of brandy. I was on the pill. We had intended to go eat after the movie. Why don't we go later, he said; why don't we sit down and get to know each other first, huh? He was staying at a hotel. We had a friendly chat. Let's move a little closer together, huh? It's easier to talk. He was fat and pleasantly homely. Never had brandy tasted so good.

I don't want to. Nono, don't be afraid. I'm not gonna do anything. But it's fun to snuggle up close a little, dontcha think? The drops of brandy cling to the roof of my mouth, flow together, then trickle down my throat and explode inside me. I don't want to. Everything has grown heavy and sluggish. My legs are stuck together; I can't move them. I feel his weight upon me, burdensome tons on top of the heavy brandy. He is cursing, I keep throwing up into the wash basin. I hadn't made it to the toilet; now all the golden brandy is in the sink. This has never happened to him before, a girl who vomits. In the subway I keep retching, through barely opened eyes I see the disgusted look on the face of an English lady sitting across from me. First look right and then left when crossing the street, not like at home. All the doors open and close automatically. At some point I wake up; it is half past two. Dammit, I'd at least like to be able to sleep it off. I grope my way to the bathroom, to wash out my things. I threw up on the faded blue. Afterward I can't get back into my room; I left the key sticking in the door from the inside. I wander through the building through streaming light empty hallways roving shadows walls doors. In the lobby I curl up on a sofa. A cool early morning breeze wafts in through the open door leading out to the garden. I can't find a blanket; my feet are getting ice cold. It won't be warm for hours. A word is roaming around in my brain. I keep trying to apply it to the preceding evening, but it doesn't fit. The evening oozes out from under it, a puddle of brown. The four letters *r a p e* drown in it.

A year later I'm driving through Berlin with Dave, whom I've been in love with for a few weeks. We have met by accident; he gives me a ride. I've just come from the ear doctor; I have an abcess, and it hurts. It is summer; I am wearing a dress.

On the way we decide we'd like to go to bed with each other and go to his place. A gentle summer breeze wafts through the open window onto my legs as we lie there, our energy spent. That's how I must have gotten a bladder infection.

On the way he keeps looking over at my bare knees, finally reaches over, touches them and asks, would I like to come home with him? (don't ever go home with a strange man! —but this is different. I love him!) I nod, we drive to his place. Something goes wrong; his penis slips out of me. Dave gets angry. My ear aches. (Does that little bit of pain matter, if he wants me!) I try very hard to position myself correctly until he gets his orgasm. A gentle summer breeze wafts through the open window, icy, onto my legs. That's how I must have gotten a bladder infection.

Circumstances do indeed color our perception of things. Love is often nothing but a shock reaction. A reaction to the shock of finding that reality is brutally different than one has imagined. Love can be a means of camouflaging brutality for awhile. Love is often nothing more than layer upon layer of dependencies of every kind, for example the dependency brought about by the need for a man's approval. One layer of love can mask dependencies for awhile. Love is perpetually mistaking being desired for being violated.

A man, who is in general a menace, is supposed to be worth loving, taken as an individual. A masculine body, which is in general dangerous, is supposed to become desirable, taken as an individual. Our every day is filled with such schizophrenia. A woman alone can hardly survive if she is not willing to disown herself. For as long as she has the patronage of one individual man, she need not worry about all the others and the threat they represent.

I was still in love with Dave, lying there in the hospital with a urinary tract infection. He regretted the fact that we wouldn't be able to go to bed with each other for awhile. I did too. I needed him because I didn't have myself.

To have a middleman, a mediator between me and the world. The more audacious and unapproachable he was, the more tightly I wove the strands of our complicity, the more I imagined "freedom and adventure." But he was the one who decided when I could go out with him; he opened and closed the doors to the world. I stood at the window waiting for the return of the solitary, battle-weary hero. No matter whether he returned exhausted from work, from union meetings, from football, from too much thinking or suntanned from vacation: I took him in, tended to his needs, gave him strength. Full of inner virtues, layer upon layer. Silent and sensual, sympathetic and compassionate.

"You're not possessive," said Dave. "That's rare in a woman." No practice, no prior history in speaking, no demands. Being able to speak, a mute wish.

A world apart, the calming inner world. The division between internal and external is reestablished daily. The division of labor has penetrated everything, has permeated the very marrow of even the most revolutionary of comrades / what is revolutionary? He is not about to do anything to change this condition—his penis is at stake. Hearth and home are no longer necessary as tokens of this division between the internal and external. The conditioning goes deeper than that.

> Women are better people
> than men, Dave maintained, they are
> more democratic, more humane, more diplomatic
> All women are beautiful! He also said:
> You must begin the revolution
> Left to themselves men will change
> nothing. They have too much to do.

Beneath the surface of my skin, new cracks were forming. I noticed them at once but did nothing about them. I was fascinated yet unsure of what to do, even though I had the feeling that I was about to be ravaged once again.

The first winter in Berlin was long and unusually cold. I arrived laden with a sense of self-awareness, the unmistakable need to withdraw. I had lost the knack of intercourse, once so painfully acquired. The frenzy of the first love a distant failure, perished in hatred. Never again would I become so deeply involved with another human being! Quite a while back I had given up the idea of marriage. It was "bourgeois."

Into the jungle of the cities, to be in the midst of it all! I resolved never to expose myself to devastation again. Feelings were sentimental . . . no more sentimentality, no more pain. Ines and I agreed that we had become cautious. We were more selective, no longer as generous in bestowing our affection. We wanted to demystify sexuality. It was to be considered a casual matter, no longer the highpoint of an encounter with another person but, rather, a superficial means of getting to know each other.

The alarm clock scared me to death every morning. The washcloth was often frozen solid. Ines was attending the university; she had the ideas. I had the alarm clock. How swiftly we found ourselves growing apart again, our life-styles so different! It took only a few weeks. Ines had imagination; I had a living to earn. My sedentary instinct prevailed. You should get your degree, she said. Three years—that's nothing!

Ines would get up only after I had already stumbled out of the house and raced for the bus. The sun began to warm the basement apartment. Now she could turn on the radio, eat breakfast, get the heat going, straighten up, and sit down at the table in front of the window, time to think, time to be productive.

The affair with Nadjenka had her coming and going, had both of them coming and going. She hardly spoke of it. She cloaked herself in an impenetrable layer of you-don't-know-anything-about-it, you-can't-understand-it. She was withdrawn more often than before. Sometimes her face betrayed traces of resignation, bitterness, yet the fire in her eyes blazed all the stronger. Whenever she returned from West Germany, lacerated by a visit to Nadjenka, this fire in her eyes was mixed with anger and despair. She tried to encroach upon Nadjenka's marital terrain; she did not succeed. Through the icy mist surrounding me, I stared at them intently. It really was happening all over again; I couldn't believe my eyes. It was like watching a movie. Everything seemed familiar, their longings pains the madness of it all. I was overcome by nostalgic craving for things far away, it was painful—were feelings still possible? The nights were short, my sleep shallow and troubled. My loneliness became unbearable. In a strange city, lacking the strength to seek people out. The love these two women felt for each other was omnipresent. After the initial shock of finding out that it really was true, it became an accepted fact. I knew the people well.

I thought about the conversation I had had with Nadjenka while still in Bern. I kept looking at her throughout the conversation, not knowing why I was so attracted to her. When she can really laugh, Nadjenka laughs as if in flight. Her long blond hair flies away with her; her teeth outshine the clouds. While we were talking, I felt the brownish skin on her neck leaving an indelible impression within me. Without admitting it to myself, I knew that I could lose myself in it—I would not give in to such a notion, not at that time at least! The feeling of being already acquainted with it, of already knowing about it from before, became stronger as time passed.

"It's not your fault that you're white," said Dave.

My hands had been the intermediary for our meeting. The good hands of women, they soothe the worries of men, they bring up the children.

Dave had no medical insurance, no money, needed some treatment. I wanted to get to know him. Over at his place I did the same thing I did all day long in the clinic: I restored that which was ailing. Dissipated energy, bruised feelings. Women's great healing power degenerates in the service of inhumane hospitals and exploitative couple relationships based on dependency. I can't remember a man ever brushing the cares from my forehead with a gentle hand as I had done countless times. Even after a full day's work, physically exhausted, I still had a tender hand to caress the forehead of the man saddled with worries and cares.

At first Dave's racism escaped me. For weeks we had our eyes on each other. Sometimes we would joke about going to bed together someday. He was much more in touch with his body than most whites and was convinced that their sensuality had atrophied. If my sensuality goes too, what would be left? When we finally slept together, I gave him free rein. I would prove to him that the sensuality of this white woman had not withered away.

The old sage had two treatment rooms in a large Spanish-style building with an inner courtyard. His hands were endowed with healing powers. Everyone who came to him he massaged thoroughly, taking a long time, until they felt whole again. The treatment couch stood in the smaller of the two rooms. An archway led into the adjacent room, which was empty.

I went to him because I didn't know any other way out. As he massaged me with his warm hands, a lion that belonged to him sat at the other side of the couch. He was an extraordinarily beautiful, powerful animal. His coat and mane brushed against my body throughout the treatment. Afterward I cradled his head in both hands and stroked it firmly along the sides. Nothing in the world could have disturbed my equilibrium.

Dave was waiting for me outside. Before leaving I wanted to go into the larger room, into which the lion had withdrawn. I wanted to look at him all by myself, without the old man. The lion fascinated me so much that I would have liked nothing better than to take him home with me. The large room was separated from the hallway by a purple curtain. The heavy velvet absorbed all noises, thoughts, and feelings, severed every connection with the world outside. The old man sat motionless in the small room, oblivious to his surroundings.

The lion raised his head as I entered the room. Away from the old man he became a savage beast of prey again and tried to attack me as I slowly turned back, panic-stricken. I wanted to cry for help, but the purple curtain smothered the sound in my throat. I kept taking the same step forward without being able to budge.

At that moment a little black kitten padded into the old man's room. She was quite naive, a bit wily, and had an incredibly silken, gleaming coat. I liked her instantly, but in comparison to the lion, she seemed insignificant. When he discovered her, he was immediately distracted, and I could get away. This dream, unlike any other, haunted me for years. Its presence was sometimes intense, sometimes muted. The lion gradually lost its captivating power. The kitten—that is to say, my sexuality—came to the fore. After I had started to lead a different life, I could remember the lion and comfort him without falling under his spell.

At this time I realized that Nadjenka's fair hair had grazed the periphery of my existence for a long time.

This boundary was crumbling.

I spent the following years in the valley of slumbering women and once again fed my own heart to a black man and to a white one.

*

Nadjenka regarded me pensively.

"You love Dave too much," she asserted. "It bothers me that you love him so much."

She was here visiting Ines once again. Ines was still trying to persuade Nadjenka to come live in Berlin. She had already found an apartment and painted it when Nadjenka said no, or, rather, made it clear that she had never said yes. She was afraid of clinging too closely to Ines, afraid that she would, in the initial fear of starting out on her own, become too dependent on her.

Curiosity and fascination alone—whether aroused by skin color race nationality one's own or the opposite sex—are not enough to make one act humanely. The pleasure one human being finds in another is not independent from the current social context, nor is it separate from historical and cultural origins. From the very first moment of their encounter individuals share in all of the collective struggles past and present. From the outset the tyranny of whites over blacks, the tyranny of men, white and black, over women, the tyranny of heterosexuals over homosexuals, drive a wedge between them, create a rupture that cannot be mended no matter how hard they may try to pretend they are the only two people in this world. The burden of history, unsurmounted, unremembered, thrusts itself between them. One on one, they fight out collectively conceived battles in highly concentrated form.

Even though blacks may be more in touch with their bodies than many whites and may, by virtue of this, awaken the long lost sensuality of whites, that does not necessarily mean that it is more enjoyable to sleep with a black man, nor does it even mean that, because of his own oppression, he will treat a woman like a human being. A victim of oppression does not necessarily treat other victims of oppression more humanely. The millenial geneaology in which woman upon woman, head bowed, filled with compassion, bends over a man of stone, is made up of black white yellow brown men and women. *Sexism runs deeper than racism than class struggle.*

"How should I begin? What should I do?"

At the beginning of the development customarily termed "politicization," one that commenced with information from Ines, readings from Marcuse and now from Cleaver and Malcolm X, I sat on Dave's bed and asked, "What should I *do?*"

He glanced up from his book for a second. "Support the Black Panther party!"

As I approached him, he got up from his desk deep in thought. I had been showering. He had been thinking.

"You know, maybe I really don't care that much about other people," he brooded. "But sometimes I do need warmth and a little lubrication." A person who needs warmth and lubrication—what can you say to that?

The need for warmth and lubrication—sex—had become autonomous, isolated from the human being with whom these needs were to be fulfilled. This grasping for warmth and sex (not for warmth and affection) was the same as a grasping at things that were tangible and usable—quite independent of human beings: a book, a hot bath, a walk. When coupled with impatient directives (pull your legs up / open your mouth) and the inability to express one's feelings, the realization of these needs becomes all the more brutal.

A man can always void his emotional vacuity into the vagina of a woman without his perceiving her as a person, without her essentially being able to defend herself, to escape being dependent on him. Intercourse is the price she pays for security, safety, societal acceptance.

Dave fought against the tyranny of whites over blacks and yet continuously recreated the tyranny of men over women.

"I prefer being with women," said Samuel. "When I look around and see how this society is structured—everything from the unions to the police all the way up to the medical association, nothing but men—it's absolutely disgusting."

"Stop it, Samuel!" I interrupt him, "you're starting to sound like a real man-hater!"

"Gee," said Samuel, "I didn't mean it to sound that way."

Earlier on he never would have come up with the notion of a "society of men." We are discussing the fact that women and men relate to each other in a destructive way, that this destructive behavior nowhere shows itself more ingrained than in their sexuality.

I learned that changes can come about only after sexuality has been suspended for a long time and only after women learn to love other women and men other men.

When will men begin to talk to other men about their personal lives, begin, when in need of the warmth of another human being, to touch other men? That's where women come in. Women are thrust between men who, if left to themselves, would maul one another. Women talk with women and men. If they prefer the company of other women, they are immediately branded man-haters. Liking women is defined by men as hating men. But it is the men who are the ones who refuse to relate to other men, the ones who act like they hate men.

"You can't really expect me to share my private life with a man!" Samuel said defensively.

Why do they expect that of women?

This societal structure makes Samuel suffer. It makes it difficult for him to be in touch with other people. He doubts himself. This society drives him to despair. He likes being with women. It bothers him that men predominate in the public sphere. The atmosphere improves as soon as women appear on the scene.

Men's glances assault me, claw their way into the creases of my jeans between my legs as I descend the stairs to the subway. Whistles and clacking tongues cling to me. In the evening all the bruisings of the day under the shower under the skin. Cars slowing down, windows rolled down, skid marks. A lone woman, still an alien, and still up for grabs.

Whether at war or in peace, we exist in a state of emergency.

The master of the world sits opposite me in the subway. Four men on a seat that has room for five, legs sprawled, padded shoulders, hands resting on their knees, fingers spread apart. To my right and my left, male legs, firmly planted. I am sitting close up to myself, knees pressed tightly together. Women are supposed to keep their legs together. They are only supposed to spread them for the total stranger called gynecologist, and for the man with whom woman shares her bed. The rest of the time legs are supposed to be kept together. The appropriate muscles are to be held tensed all day long. I close my eyes. To cast off this repressive posture! To act as though I could sit *unhassled* with legs relaxed. I ride the subway only with my eyes closed.

Day and night, countless times, I am infringed upon. This is not my world. In this world I do not want equality. I do not want to be an equal partner in any man's brutality and degeneracy.

Positive change in human relationships will not come about until women are individually so strong that they will collectively become powerful.

"Women are every nation's niggers." This was my battle cry as I set out with Simone de Beauvoir's *Second Sex* and Valerie Solonas's *Manifesto* under my arm. Through experience I knew the horrors of patriarchal society long before I realized that I lived in a society ruled by a capitalist economy. Learning about political economy did nothing to diminish terror or sexism. Although I began to have a new perspective on work and working conditions, demands and consumption, upheavals, wars of liberation, world politics, I myself was treated the same as always.

"You're just like all the rest," said Dave, when I told him I was through with him. "You're running away—that's not very emancipated."

Emancipated?

I had been battered. Emancipation, up to now, meant becoming the mirror image of male degeneracy, meant disdainfully renouncing as banal and sentimental my feelings and pains and thoughts.

I must get away from here.

I must first of all reach myself. I had set out to conquer the world, and every step of the way I stumbled over men. I bought a notebook and worked my way through *The Second Sex*. It was finally there, in black and white, something that pertained to me. I was livid. I wanted instantaneous revolution. If men wouldn't concede that, they would just end up embroiled in an inner civil war . . .

How would they then manage to be strong on the outside?

Who created this society that hates women.
Who strung this fear
in liana vines through the streets, so that we
become entangled in them and perish in the night.

Who has the power?
A few capitalists, men say (it's irrelevant,
they say, that these capitalists are men) it's
imperialism, men say, which we must fight.

The first colonization
in the history of mankind was that
of women by men. For thousands of years
we have lived in common ghettos
in exile to this very day.
Our paths prescribed, fenced in. The difference
between the first and the second and the third world
is insignificant.
Here we have access to our kitchens,
our children's sandboxes, department stores,
laundromats, a café and the movies—

and yet during the day
we cannot walk the streets without being annoyed
cannot go alone to the parks, and where
do we eat when we're hungry
at midnight
alone?

Who should have the power?
The working class, men say, the workers.
We live off their labor; they carry our
load, they say. Whose body is used
to promote the coffee the worker drinks
before he goes to work? Who
prepared it, and who gave
birth to and cares for
the worker's children? Whose smile is used
to make the toothpaste I use—for the sake of my
kisses and not my teeth—appealing?
The soap I use to bathe—even it
is borne to market on my sisters' skin.

Rape carries a life sentence—for *me:*
I have to reckon with it for as long as I live.
And I happen to live
in a part of the world where I am not as brutally
violated as my sister in Vietnam.
But I *am* violated: even nonviolation
is defined by men. For Vietnam the saying goes:
   this is my rifle (GI holds up M-16)
   this is my gun (puts hand at crotch)
   one is for killing
   the other for fun.
and here the saying is:
   "Ich trinke täglich meinen Jägermeister,
   damit mir die kleinen, spitzen Schreie
   besser gelingen."*

---

*Advertising slogan for "Jägermeister," a German brandy, in the magazine STERN; it
means roughly, "I drink my Jägermeister every day, so that I can make the right noises
at the right time."

No one will put rats in my vagina,
like they do to my sisters in Chile.
I only hear about that.
Tomorrow it may be different.
The patriarchy plays a variety of games,
but everywhere they are directed
against women and children the old and the weak,
against all who want to live,
rather than just survive.

Battered shadow skin
yet still skin
broken skin
yet it still holds us together somehow.

Others are worse off. Does that mean we're well off?
Others are already killed
are we alive?
So many scars. So little pain.
Not even close to an answer.

"I want to come home with you," I said. Samuel wanted to
drive me home. "If you don't mind."
I debated with myself for a long time.
I am covered with scars; I have shed my old skin many times.

One of them kissed passionately, madly, so that I
felt teeth, nothing but teeth—
and I kissed passionately, madly.
Another kissed gently and thought anything else
adolescent and immature—
and I kissed gently, mature.
One of them likes my legs together, another spread
and prone, another open and wrapped round his
back—
and I kept my legs together or spread and prone or
open and wrapped round his back.
One of them wanted to keep going all night, another
could only get it on once—
And I kept going all night long or could only get
it on once.

One of them only wanted copulation; another found
that less important—
and I always copulated or found that less important.
One of them could only fall asleep in his own bed,
another had to turn away, another wanted to
cuddle close—
And I slept only in my bed or turned away
or cuddled close.

I now found myself looking for a human man. At that time
the idea of being alone seemed unbearable. This fear of being alone
was something new to me, but I didn't take the time to really
analyze it.

The further I ventured out into the world, the older I got, the
more I lost touch with myself. My curiosity and enthusiasm waned. I
moved more timidly than before, felt more constrained. The unpleasant encounters and experiences in the world outside mush-
roomed inside me, threatened to tear me apart. Those were the years
when I had to put up with further injury, yet at the same time,
unnoticed, I hoarded more and more of myself.

I was stockpiling myself.

Whenever I loved a man, I was bewildered right from the very
start. I wanted him to approve of me. If he did, I didn't believe him. I
myself loved me less than before.

Nadjenka was still in West Germany. She couldn't tear herself
away. We had gotten to the point of kissing each other. There had
been no other sexual relations between us. Our eroticism was more
important for mutual understanding; it was just like breathing,
essential for existence.

I couldn't imagine myself with any other woman. I wanted a
man who would treat me as well as Nadjenka. I wanted at last to find
sanctuary in the arms of a man.

I gather up my courage. "I want to come home with you."

The music stops. Berlin is a lunar landscape.

Samuel stares straight ahead. He finally lets out a long, drawn-
out yes. I start feeling cold. We're still driving. I see the endless road
before me, the road I must take to get to him.

When I met Samuel, I found in him a sincere human being. He
radiated warmth and sensuality. I assumed it would be possible for
us to meet each other halfway. Now his features had hardened; his

warmth had vanished. Why am I going with him just the same? I am in love / Am I in love?

I needed to get to know him. I didn't question my clutching at a night spent together. In spite of all the wounds that had left their mark, one part of me was secretly proud that I had finally reached the point of being able to go to bed with a man without making a big deal out of it.

The light in the elevator is very bright. I take a good look at Samuel. He takes a step toward me and kisses me on the mouth. We don't know each other, don't know anything about each other. Our lightheartedness has vanished, left back among the throng of people in a crowded bar. We face each other alone. In a few minutes we will take our clothes off and lie down together in one bed. This kiss cannot belie what we are about to do. We stand there face to face. He puts his hand on my shoulder. I smile up at him. He looks down on me. He puts his arm around me. I lean on him. He pulls me close. I cling to him.

Total silence. Craters open up. The elevator jerks to a halt.

In the apartment Samuel takes me by the hand and says, Come on, let's have another drink. Warily, we look each other over in the neon kitchen light. With whom are we getting involved? It seems we cannot recognize each other. It is an awkward situation for both of us. In his room he lies down on the bed, clasps his hands behind his head and looks at me. He flutters helplessly with clipped feelings.

I begin to close the distance between us. Hesitantly I begin to move, placing one foot in front of the other. My face is smiling. I keep hoping that he will come and meet me half-way after all. I wait for him to make the first move, I don't rush him don't make demands of him give him time. All along the equator around the globe I move steadily toward him as our bodies already start into motion. With practiced hands we undress each other. The signals are getting through. Arms and legs and torso in motion. A surface bombardment of familiar tactics, we stretch, bend, turn, get up, lie back. At last we can close our eyes. Our lips kiss. Searching hands try to do more than merely trace the familiar lines along the body of the opposite gender, try to truly reach the person beneath that surface. We try to laugh, silently try to fabricate a bit of happiness.

From books films and experiences that affirmed that which we know from books and films, we know what she/he wants. We act and react accordingly. We react to her/his knowing what he/she wants.

We count on that which we know from books and films and experiences indeed being accurate.

Samuel has made his way to my breasts. They remain lifeless. I still don't love them. How dreadful that pleasure can arise even though I don't love myself, even though love of self and love of another are detached from each other, like talk and love, like work and love, like pleasure and love.

He bows his head; at last he can rest it for a moment. I take him in. Once again I look down on a man's head nestling between my breasts. What is he searching for?

I start running, Samuel disappears, the distance separating us remains the same. Is Samuel a mirage? Is my need to be nurtured a mirage? I would like to put a stop to this at once, would like to move away from him, look him in the eyes, talk to him, fall asleep with him. Is my vagina moist? Is his penis hard? Have all the preparations been made for reuniting the disunited? Vagina-penis has become a surrogate unity, a substitute for all severed relationships.

His penis is moving in my vagina. It slid in smoothly. It doesn't seem to be a long one, my right ovary doesn't hurt. His penis is moving in my vagina even before I can reach Samuel, the one to whom it belongs. My first wave of passion has long since receded, abated. Samuel's face relaxes. It is this damned genital solemnity that I have never been able to comprehend.

The fact that I did not have an orgasm is a topic studiously avoided, just like the question of what an orgasm actually is. "All this talk about being a sex object! I don't think it's so bad satisfying each other sexually, do you?"

To postpone for a few seconds the icy death, to interrupt the anonymity and aloneness:

To become flesh.

To be recognized by someone, to get the feeling of really existing as a person, singular and unique:

To become flesh.

We know all the rules. Sometimes, perhaps, contentment drapes the windows. Once more we have been spared. Samuel lifts his head one more time: it really is nicer to fall asleep with somebody. My head nods. My hand strokes his hair: his face rests under my arm. My eyes fill the darkness.

By morning the apparition has vanished. Two comrades, one female and one male, meet again in the kitchen of a commune in

Berlin. That which remains: to find out why I did not stay away after that first night, after those first signs that here, too, hard labor, perhaps even annihilation, awaited me.

I was a woman of average intelligence,
twenty-three years of age,
under the influence of neither alcohol
nor drugs nor tranquilizers.
I was financially independent,
neither married to the man, nor did I
have nor expect a child from him.
There were no extraneous circumstances compelling me
    to write with him a chapter of shared history and even
  – against his will – to move into his apartment

That's too complicated for me
You can't take any criticism
Your subjectivity will get you nowhere
You're not at all well
    Those things you write with your friends are shocking
You're driving yourselves further and further
                                        into isolation.
I worry about you
You're getting further and further off the track
Again we are talking about Feminism,
weren't we going to talk about us

    You mean more to me than
                        anything in the world.

I was a poor sister to myself.

Many an evening I spent in a bar with loquacious Marxists, unable to contribute anything to their conversation. I didn't know enough. I didn't have the courage to ask questions. "So-and-so is another one of those who was incredibly sensitized by the student movement . . ."

The new humanity? I remained a mere listener. Samuel spent the night with me and then, next morning, continued his discussions with the sensitized Marxist who came to breakfast.

To love a comrade—despite his membership in a particular faction—did not change my situation in any way. Sometimes he even refused to talk to me. Sometimes he didn't display any affection at all, yet his gray matter became dysfunctional as soon as I broached the subject of the oppression of women—in his brain nothing but a vague concept.

He does not deny that there is such a thing; he is informed. He has a vague idea that women are being terrorized by force and fear. His feelings of collective guilt weigh heavily upon him.

"I don't terrorize women!" he shouts indignantly, when I tell him how I am constantly ogled and harassed. All his intelligence, his powers of abstract reasoning, his great knowledge, fail him when we are on this subject. He becomes entangled in a muddle of thoughts and feelings. He is no longer capable of distinguishing between personal situations and circumstances in general. In especially difficult and deplorable cases, he claims that women *want* to be raped. In this way he can get rid of some of his guilt feelings and justify his complacency and lack of concern.

This is the reaction I get when I talk about the situation of women in general. But when I confront him personally, his own misdirected emotions come to the fore. Why don't you wipe that snot right off your nose! is what I hear. Why don't you stop whining! It's not such a big deal.

The terrors of sexuality have long been operating autonomously. They will persist, in spite of economic upheavals, unless we do something about them.

"I am terribly fond of you."

This first measly concession came the evening before Samuel left on vacation, half a year after we had wordlessly slept with each other for the first time. He could hardly say the words, so exhausted was he from keeping his defenses up. The pending vacation made it easier for him to make such an admission. I had waited patiently, had become cautious, oh so masochistically cautious. The time that I told Dave I loved him, he burst into laughter. "Love, that's something for kids," he said. Even being black did not change that. So Samuel's modest admission touched me, and I felt gratified. My investment had paid off at last; my efforts had not gone unnoticed. How often I had been at the point of giving up, dissolved in tears. ("Come on, you act like you're going to die!" he would say.)

What an effect such a sentence has, when it comes from the mouth of an unapproachable man! Once again his sexism appears to be nothing more than a personal problem, one removed from all cultural and political considerations. Woman, filled with compassion, perceives it as mere human frailty. At times like this she almost invariably concludes that she has not yet humanized him adequately, that it is her own personal duty to change masculine behavior; she does not think in terms of a Cultural Revolution.

Work at the hospital was so taxing that in our free time—much of which was of course taken up by political activities—Samuel and I just barely managed to organize our daily routine enough to keep our heads above water. Though on the average we had four nights a week booked up, we still felt the need to sit down and read once in awhile, the need to see friends, to keep in touch with things; this left us with maybe an hour on the weekend to ourselves—usually spent in intercourse. Whenever we spent a bit of time together in public, we rationed ourselves: we didn't actually relate to each other; we were simply *there* next to each other—out drinking, eating, taking a walk, at the movies. We hardly spoke to each other. We went through the familiar motions but had neither the time nor the energy to question them or weigh their implications: bewilderment, loss, adjustment.

I used up a lot of energy just keeping my separate lives from falling apart. I had guilt feelings about the plight of the working class. I had guilt feelings about Samuel.

I identified with the women from "Bread ♀ Roses" and with their projects. Ever since that evening when one of the women had come to talk to Samuel about the pill and the pharmaceutical industry, my various lives had become entangled. My work with these women had become much more than just another weekly meeting. When I started working with them on "Frauenhandbuch Nr. 1," I had been out of work for three months, waiting to get my first job at the hospital. I was able to devote all my time to the group. Not for a long time had I been so intensively, so thoroughly, so integrally, involved with something that was not divorced from myself, something that did not engender this sense of estrangement. Now I had finally overcome the feeling that had originated long ago when I was still reading a lot.

I shared my apartment and my sexuality with Samuel. I earned my money at the clinic. I thought, worked, learned, and felt at ease with the women of "Bread ♀ Roses." I encountered the women's *issue* through the women themselves; it was not something divorced, removed from them. I was drawn to these women, their radiance, their diverse, distinctive life-styles.

At first I would leave Samuel to attend a woman's meeting only to come back again to the life with him. Gradually the emphasis shifted. I came back less and less.

Nadjenka is pregnant. After my tonsillectomy I go to visit her in West Germany. Knees shaking, I walk down the long platform at the train station. She is not here. I walk slowly through the turnstile, put my luggage on a bench. She is not inside the station either. She had missed me among the arriving passengers and had gone to the stationmaster: "She must have been on this train; she has to be here." When I catch sight of her, she is out of breath. Walking has become difficult for her. Her flaxen hair is piled on top of her head; her eyes are bleary. We go for some ice cream. The plush furniture in the café feels sticky in the hot sun. "How would I ever have described you to the stationmaster?" she says, "your face has gotten even thinner, and you are so pale . . ."

My eyes hurt for a moment to see her in that condition. Now she is trapped for good, I think to myself. I don't understand why she wants to have a child. She can't tell me either. I had been there on another visit when she got word from the doctor. "Yes, I am pregnant," she said bruskly, a defiant look on her face, "and I want the child."

My misgivings made not the slightest impression on her.

"Finally something in my life which I am responsible for," she said, "someone to give me a reason to live . . ."

Why don't you come to Berlin? Over the years this wish had lurked beneath the surface—the child would mean it would never come true. "You're right," said Nadjenka, "the child will protect me from you too, protect me from the leap into a new life . . ."

How shocked I was to find out she was a married woman! I had met her as an individual woman, and, even after I knew she was married, I could never conceive of her being a married woman. Even when I saw her with her husband, my perception of her remained essentially the same; she didn't suddenly become one half of a couple. Yet one evening at dinner in a restaurant, I was taken aback: she was sitting not across from *me*, but next to him.

The web of do-you-still-remember and back-when-we-were-engaged intimacies was spun between the plates and bowls on the table. These were meaningless intimacies, yet she unwittingly wove these threads anew time and time again. She never cut through the nexus of the web. She only attempted to unravel individual threads and in the process became more and more entangled.

Nadjenka's territory begins behind the apartment building. Wind is there, sky trees fields and meadows. As always, I look on in amazement as she shows me the paths of her life, her stopping places, secret hideaways, things she cares about. There is a nursery where she goes to get her flowers, animals she knows are running about. Here and there she finds carrots or radishes left behind in the fields and picks them up. I talk about meetings, appointments, about circulating leaflets. She talks about the other women in the building, about circulating questionnaires for a public opinion poll.

I watch her while she pares vegetables. She holds an onion in the palm of her hand. She fingers it for a few moments before peeling and slicing it. How is it that Nadjenka has the time to hold an onion in her hand long enough for the sensation of it to actually leave behind a momentary impression? There are more pressing things, time itself is more pressing; it presses continuously; there is so much to be done.

"I don't use the same board anymore for cutting fruits and vegetables," she says, interrupting my thoughts. "Once I put my nose to it, you wouldn't believe it, that combination of banana and onion was disgusting."

Is that important? Is it revolutionary? When will the right time have come for learning to savor aromas?

"What is so strange about me?" she asks me on the street, turning to face me. "Everybody says I don't fit into the mold. Do you think I am different from everybody else too?"

Why do you look at me that way, I cannot help you. My lips, the corners of my mouth trembling; I say, "Yes, you are different, but what it is, I cannot tell. Why does it bother you?"

Can you hear me? Are you bending over the bathtub, washing something? Do you hurt all over again; are you going up against the whole town all alone again? Why don't you seek out other women? "There aren't any!" you maintain. "I wasn't even able to set up a child care co-op."

"What's going on," asks Samuel hesitantly, "what's going on between Nadjenka and you? Did you go to bed with her?"

All I wanted was to lie there quietly and inhale her. To hold onto this warmth that has no other motive than to warm. Then it *is* possible for people to touch each other this way, I thought with amazement. Our hands' only mission to caress belly and hips, back and legs, lingering in every curve and hollow. The covers tented in the ascending warmth. Nadjenka's flaxen hair streaming through the mist. The down on her tanned cheeks seemed lighter as our lips came together and explored the contours of our mouths. The silken palate and mellow membrane melted on our tongues. We stopped in our enraptured exchange of droplets of saliva only long enough to return to nestling in each others' lips.

"Yes and no," I tell Samuel, "it's not like what you think, I can't explain it."

And I add immediately: "The best thing would be if we could all be bisexual."

Samuel takes his pipe out of his mouth. "What are you getting at? I mean, I could never sleep with a man, even the thought of it gives me the creeps. You like women, that I can still understand, but me with a man? . . ."

Did I really want to be bisexual? Wasn't it really my fear of hurting Samuel, of rejecting him, which made me say that? Was it a belief in the utopian idea that bisexuality was a feasible life-style, not only a depreciated sexual alternative but a whole new way of life?

"We put such restrictions on each other," I said to him. "The whole time Nadjenka was here visiting she slept alone in my bed; I slept in the next room with you. Our world would have collapsed if I had spent even one night with her and you had to sleep by yourself. It wouldn't have mattered whether we had talked, made love, or just lain next to each other–it would have been totally out of the question for us to spend the night together. We two leftists are not that far removed from Nadjenka's marital relationship. We are so tied to each other that I don't dare do such a thing, and Nadjenka's mere presence makes you feel threatened."

"I really prefer being together with women," Samuel says once again.

"Yeah, me too," I reply. "I know what you mean."

"I just hope that won't turn out to be a problem," Samuel says.

I was tired of sexuality.

For me it was a question of rewriting my own falsified history. After a group meeting I always wanted to stay on and continue the discussion. I wanted to press on, thinking differently, living differently, I did not want to have to justify, explain, interpret my actions.

"You're not giving me a chance," says Samuel. "You don't credit me with the ability to change."

Solidarity was the big issue for him now. When had I ever shown solidarity with myself? The strength of women was important to me, not that of men. I was interested in women's anxieties, not those of men. I wanted to figure out in my own mind what would happen if women broke free of men.

These roles have made it impossible for people to recognize one another.

What is the most effective and fastest way to abolish them?

I wanted to find out what it would mean to be alone, what the absence of sexuality, the absence of a steady relationship with any one particular person, would mean.

Withdrawal Symptoms

"I am practicing living without you," says Samuel. "Every morning when I get up alone and stand there in the bathroom all alone, I tell myself, I can make it without her."

We did not split up. I simply moved out. Three women, each having shed her former life with a man, decided to share an apartment.

I am optimistic. Surrounded as I am by the women in my group and the women in the apartment, occupied by the work of the group, by new ideas and prospects, the pain of cutting the umbilical ties to Samuel does not surface until later. Now when I curl up in one corner of the bed to sleep, I am convinced that I don't need much more in life than one such quiet corner. Solitude is therapeutic.

Even after moving, the separation from Samuel is a constant struggle waged anew in each verbal encounter. Samuel does not belong to any group. He is lonely and has neither the desire nor ability to experience loneliness. He is afraid of growing old alone.

While I was moving out, I kept turning around to look back at him. During the first few days I went back several times, and during the first week I spent more nights in Samuel's bed than in my own.

I am giving up an intimacy acquired at great cost. It seems to have become irreplaceable. I am breaking loose from a chapter of shared history. I am on intimate terms with the terrors of the present, but the unknown future harbors unforeseeable dangers. Even though the dissension between us may have become intolerable, the recollection of shared intimacies seems to outweigh the intolerable moments. There seems to be a stronger sense of abandonment outside than inside this intolerable state. I know that Samuel cares for me. . . . (He has changed so much! an acquaintance said to me. Now you want to leave him?) My knowing this does not make my decision wrong, but it does make it more difficult to carry out.

Samuel rests his burdened head on his hands.

"We are practicing separation," he says. "You have to keep proving to me that you don't need me, that you can live without me. You don't want to admit that things aren't going well for you. I'm only human too; I can only take so much . . ."

"I'm not trying to prove anything," I counter emphatically. We are trying to reach an understanding. Yet after years of scarcely being able to understand or even recognize each other, years of only leaning on each other, our sole attraction skin to skin, we do not know how to start coming to terms with each other now. After almost three years we have reached the point where we can no longer say things merely for the sake of saying them. We ponder, weigh our words carefully. We are already lugging around too many abortive attempts; we are burdened by too much familiarity.

A great deal is at stake.

Samuel wants to talk so that he can cling to the faint hope that one day I might want to come back to him. He imagines my mind to be in a state of chaos. He wants to find out what is going on inside of me, why I no longer want to share his life.

I did share it right from the very beginning.

Just to be near him I trotted around everywhere with him, from the meeting places and bars in the leftist ghetto to the late showings of wild west films. Samuel did not show the least bit of interest in me. If it had been up to him alone, we would not have spent any time together. As soon as people noticed me, word got around that Samuel had a new girlfriend. Look! a shadow that regularly and unfailingly accompanies him wherever he goes. How odd to see Samuel with the same woman month after month! I moved into his circle, leaving my old one behind.

I want to talk in order to gain acceptance of my new ideas.

I am just beginning to live them; I do not have much to report as yet. Exasperated, I want to rid him of the idea that "doing only feminist stuff" is trivial. His facility with words impedes me. I hear a torrent of didactics in a language that will never be adequate for my purposes.

I begin to talk, while Samuel expectantly draws on his pipe. There is a sentence imprinted on my mind—you talk so slowly that by the time you've finished I've already forgotten where you started! — but no matter how I speak, hesitantly or fluently, whether I use my own words or the inadequate leftist jargon, as I offer explanation after explanation trying to clarify, as I send message after message trying to explain my new life, my words do not get through to him; they get lost somewhere before reaching his ears.

I lead a different life, speak another language. Even if I knew how to translate it, I would not be interested in expending my energies this way. I find that we have nothing more in common. My need to fabricate something seems to be waning. I keep trying to explain only because I am dealing with a chapter in my life which was spent with Samuel. Was it all for nothing? I would like to know what we actually accomplished in the past three years, what I was trying to achieve.

"I don't know what you want," I often hear. It is true that at some point I started becoming more and more withdrawn. I led a private life hidden from the view of men. It was my reaction to the fact that they did not perceive me as a person.

I still needed a man's approval to verify my existence as a unique person, as one distinguishable from others. I had rarely had a relationship with a man without going to bed with him. Intercourse had always been important for gaining men's approval.

I watched silently and stored everything I saw and experienced inside myself. That was before I could put into words the things that offended me, the things that tore me apart. I dissolved into tears every time I struggled to make myself understood. Gradually I began to recognize the facts and situations that I did *not* like.

When I finally opened my mouth the patterns were there in my mind: of all the things I learned to express, the most difficult was the word *no*.

Its predecessors had been:
Actually . . . I didn't
you know, I think that
I merely meant to say
what I meant was
do you understand what I mean?

Samuel recognizes that he is no longer the most important thing in my life. This gives him a mental block.

"I am not trying to prove anything," I repeat. "My life has changed. I can live without you. In my head certain patterns have disintegrated, and in yours they are still intact."

Changes really are taking place *here and now;* we do not have to wait for "day x." We are alarmed to see a *private* upheaval taking place. We do not believe in this, we do not want that, it is tedious and unpleasant. It is easier to talk about how difficult it is to bring about such private upheavals than it is to find oneself in the throes of one that had been contemplated. It is easier to support upheavals that take place far removed from your own life sphere than it is to leave your own shell, easier to be affected by struggles far removed from one's own self than it is to start from where one is personally affected. Even the leftists have relegated the personal sphere to a position of secondary importance.

"Are you happier now?" asks Samuel. "Was it really so awful when we were together? What was so awful, and, if it was so awful, then why did you stay?"

Six months before that I had returned from a two-week vacation spent in Italy with two women from "Bread ♀ Roses." I had never yet gone on vacation with Samuel. The separate vacations—really a vacation from couplehood—served as a shaky bulwark against exclusivity. It was a faint reminder of the fact that we still did not know how to regard our life together. We had become lethargic, virtually paralyzed.

For a long time now we had been stuck in the same groove, moving on parallel tracks, leaning up against each other. Once Samuel started openly acknowledging our relationship, we did have good times together. We said we loved each other more often than we had in the past. We exhibited our affection for each other in public; it no longer embarrassed him. A difficult man had turned into a pleasant person. His friends were amazed. But in the meantime I had begun asking for more than affection and sex. Sexuality was now only a relic of the past. I had expended all my emotions. Love crumbled and fell to the ground, leaving a trail behind me, the last traces from the old world. Men no longer commanded my loyalty.

The days in Italy were filled with work. In our initial shyness we talked little about our personal lives, and yet a certain sense of well-being prevailed. I read *The Dialectic of Sex.* My head was bursting with new impulses and ideas when we arrived in Berlin. Samuel picked us up at the train station. I stood on the sidewalk and watched absently as he got out of the car. Then we smilingly approached each other and embraced. This is the man you know so well, I thought to myself, pressing my face against his rough cheek. The ground beneath me opened up.

This sense that my place was with him, on what was it really based? Why was it becoming increasingly difficult to reconcile this feeling with my sense of attachment to these women?

I was in the process of relocating myself; I wanted to lift my shoes from the groove in the track next to his. When I noticed that they'd taken root I slipped out of them and, barefoot, went on. For a long time Samuel kept standing there next to my empty shoes. He could not see which way I had turned, where I was headed, what I so fervently sought.

A comrade, a woman with whom he was working on a project, was staying with us for a few days. As soon as he got home from work they would sit down together to talk. I wanted to speak to him about my vacation, about why I felt more at home with these two women than I did living here with him, wanted to talk about what we had accomplished, what we had thought, things we had figured out. I would have been able to talk about it in the first days after I got back from vacation. For two weeks I had been able to behave differently; I felt refreshed enough to penetrate the silence between Samuel and myself.

It was not long before I had a relapse. I could not compete with the verbose exchanges between him and the other woman. She seemed able to hold her own in conversations with him. I was still trying to measure up to his erudition, his intellect. My interests were supposed to come up to his standards. A week later he finally found time for me, but by then the words had left me. I assumed that he considered my experiences insignificant. He felt threatened. He refused to read *The Dialectic of Sex.* "Why can't you just tell me what's in it that is so important?" he asked. "I don't understand how you can just plunk down a couple of books about all your problems and expect me to read them!"

I was furious. Didn't he always read up on every other important political issue, analyzing and discussing these ideas with his comrades, men and women whose opinions he valued? Why did he refuse to expend time and energy, ideas and notes, paper and pencil, when the women's issue was at stake?

To this day he refuses to read even a single line written by a feminist. Although it had affected his personal life and left its mark on him, he will not deal with this issue on an analytical level. "I don't have the time," he insists. "I can't possibly get involved in everything." "Just *tell* me what's in the book—why don't you tell me a nice bedtime story!"

Late one evening he left with this other woman to get some information from a friend. They did not ask me whether I wanted to come along. It was evident that I, as Samuel's girlfriend, had as usual only taken up space without contributing anything to the conversation. I was the one who shared his bed. Speaking, thinking, discussing, researching, those things he shared with others. The old barrier had not been lifted. Our physical communication did not facilitate a deeper understanding of each other; it was the only means we had of relating at all. The retreat into eroticism and sexuality, which stemmed from the inability to communicate and the fear of expressing one's feelings, resulted in a sexual relationship that was just as mute and devoid of emotion. My importance to him did not lie in conversations and common interests that had to do with topics and events outside our private sphere; it lay instead in the formless folds and corners of shelter and intimacy. It was enough that I was present: a fixture in his life as well as in his room.

I could not fall asleep; even the vodka did not help. The longer I thought about what I meant to Samuel, the more upset and desperate I became. When he finally returned I was wide awake and totally exhausted. I started to cry when he asked what was wrong with me. He was startled and concerned. "There isn't anything going on between me and her," he said in an attempt to calm me down. He thought I was jealous for sexual reasons, and when I denied that he refused to believe me.

I found the term *jealousy* banal like all the rest of those terms for emotion and sexuality. I could not use this term without first re-examining and redefining it. It would not have mattered to me if Samuel had slept with another woman—which was an attitude he found disconcerting. But I became incensed when before my very eyes he engaged in verbal intercourse with another woman, totally excluding me.

"Don't be upset. That doesn't mean a thing," he assured me. "You know *how much I care for you.*"

These words no longer compensate.

Intercourse is no longer a substitute for understanding.

The sanctity of nocturnal emotions makes me impatient.

I care so much for you
you've got to believe me
you are so important to me

you must know that
I need you
only with you—
Orphan's talk.

This painfully contorted, wounded look used to get to me; now it no longer evokes a response. This damned genital solemnity erupts again in all its inner fury. This deadly weighty coupling! Everything that is lacking during the day is converted at night into gravely serious actions and embryonic phrases. The nocturnal phrases are so ponderous that they carry over into the coming day, resulting in an amorphous sense of obligation.

How many years can this same scene be played, countless variations on the same theme? How can it be played throughout a lifetime? Does this confusion and inner strife at some point, unnoticed, deaden the senses until there is no longer the chance nor the strength to revolt?

My feelings were all used up. I was irritated and angry. Only when I had demands with which to confront Samuel was I able to make my move. Had I given up during the long period when it all seemed unbearable, I would only have been sentencing myself to impotence.

Should I move out, or shouldn't I? I spent most of the autumn and winter looking for an apartment. An apartment for three women. All the doors open onto one hallway. Our paths cross on the way from our rooms to the bathroom, to the kitchen, to the front door. The hallway bears the traces of three women whose lives intersect. The patterns soon become labyrinthine. The apartment was jammed to the rafters with us. Their former lives still make demands on each of them. Will the apartment be big enough?

"I am no longer a part of your life," Samuel's voice penetrates the silence. He cannot understand the new way in which he exists for me now. I regard him pensively. "You're one of my best friends," I hear myself say. This he can't stand. He does not want to be just a good friend. After all those years, including those before our life together, years in which feelings proved deceptive, love proved undefinable, sexuality proved futile, after all those years during which feelings, love, and sexuality did not help us to relate to each other as human beings, after all that time Samuel still insists upon that illusive notion of being more-than-just-a-good-friend. Now, when the time has come for a determined and thorough examination of addiction as well as dedication to work, of exclusivity as well as loneliness!

The poster on the wall of our living room visibly upsets him. Two women are pictured. One of them says: some of my best friends are men, and the other retorts: yes, but would you want your sister to marry one?

Samuel has lost his sense of direction. Now he needs me as never before. He can't make it on his own. My behavior seems to have rubbed off on him. He doesn't quite know what to do with his new feelings and needs; he has become unsure about how to handle his penis. He has learned that there is more to sexuality than copulation. He still can't accept the idea. He talks about "oral and manual satisfaction" as if referring to something dirty which one squeamishly holds at a distance. He does not talk of lips and fingertips. He does not want to accept the fact that copulation has to be put aside for a time if it is to be experienced anew and given a different priority. "I can't do without it!" he claims.

Without a vagina? Without a woman? Without people?

If I could look into his eyes *just to look into his eyes!*

If I could caress him *just to caress him!*

If I could kiss him *just to kiss him!*

If I could trace the lines of his body *just to trace the lines of his body!*

If he could lie with me *just to lie with me!*

If we would meet, in order to encounter each other,

If we would want to see each other, in order to find each other,

What a revolution!

Down with copulation!

But

Whether I look into his eyes, caress or kiss him, our hands fail to meet, they touch only emptiness. The glances splinter the moment they meet.

Blind deaf and dumb, babbling, we seek a way out of the labyrinth; we cling to each other's lips. Sucking, that we know. Blindly the penis gropes its way into the vagina. Up until this one half-hour at midnight we are separated from each other, we have hardly anything in common. That is why this common orgasm is so urgent. It makes us feel that we belong to each other, that many things unite us.

Orgasm has been blown up out of proportion. It has flattened sexuality. It is all that remains of sexuality. Everything else is forgotten, including the question of what an orgasm actually is and what significance it might have for human understanding.

All those sleepless nights have made me vigilant.

I watch the person next to me, watch myself, watch him and me during intercourse.

A body has skin and hair, folds and flesh, curves and planes. I can lift my hand and place it on the body of the person next to me. I can rest it there. It turns to stone when I think about what effect it can have on the other body. These predictable reactions make my eyes grow heavy. I am getting tired, dead tired. I curl up, cradle myself in my arms.

Now

if only I could lean on you, if you would warm me so that I could tranquilly fall asleep. I hope for dreams. The penis intervenes. Lately it has been slipping out of my vagina more often than usual. I am no longer making an effort to hold it in. In my dreams of late, planes are crashing. Planes that have just taken off fall from the sky, the gangway pushed up to the door does not fit, it slides off, the passengers cannot board. Flying has become difficult.

"Why don't you feel like it? Just having an erection is enough to give me a guilty conscience!" Samuel feels rejected. The words ring in my ears. Between my legs everything is calm and dry. The copper T has been resting in my uterus for almost a year and a half. Ever since I got it I have been bleeding more heavily; every month it lasts a week, just like when I started thirteen years ago.

"Why do you want to have it removed?" the gynecologist asks. "Do you have a *particular* reason, more *serious side effects* than . . ."

"I don't want to be bothered!" I interrupt him; beads of sweat collect on my nose. "And I insist that you make note of that in my medical record!"

"But of course," he retorts sarcastically. "The patient claims that . . ."

Intercourse, as learned and practiced, is an undertaking too inconsequential to create happiness, to learn something about the other person and oneself, to communicate with each other. An act of desperation.

I push it aside. I am withdrawing from the drug of sexuality. For nine years I've been hooked on it. Desperate dependence on this one accepted kind of sexual behavior!

My eyes are fixed on myself. The lower half of my body is beginning to adhere to the upper half.

If I use contraceptives, I get sicker than I already am. In order to be able to sleep with a man, I have to become a *patient*. Contraception has become an unsolvable problem. Myself is more important to me than union with a penis.

I am permeated with *myself*.

Whenever I see Samuel, his bullheadedness and blasé attitude infuriate me. He is worried about my development. His world, the world of thoughts, manifests itself differently to him than to me . . .

He prophesies and prognosticates like an oracle. My ideas make him fidgety. He still hasn't learned to listen. He still mistakes feminist literature for bedtime stories.

I find I can tell him less and less about my new life. With arms outstretched he sits before me, staring at me from across the table, convinced he is facing the woman he "knows." But it is *me* who is sitting there.

Will he ever try to energize the imprint I've made upon him; will he ever try to act on his own? Will he do more than merely react differently toward women? Will he make that special effort needed to bring about real change? Will he expose himself to being alone in order to examine dependency from the outside? Will he take the time and effort to discover that leading one single life differently is important for radically changing society as a whole, one single life led long before "day x" (what is "day x"?), one single life that may not bring this day about but which could bring it closer? Will he reflect upon how far one life led differently can expand before one goes mad, the feeling of suffocation in the subways, the screams in the streets?

Men wear their hair long, wear colored underwear, jewelry, and platform shoes. They use sprays and cologne. The various companies try to peddle to men the wares that used to be intended for women. The roles are left untouched. Nothing more than imitation. After we leave them, men lament. They do not want to have to be dependent on other men, not even on the ones some of us women have influenced. They want the real thing, the original, the source.

Samuel must take himself in hand. I am no longer there to counterbalance his learned, masculine behavior. Until he can be alone, until he can initiate a humane relationship with another man, he will always demand more of me than I of him, and his demands will be based upon emotions and sexuality.

I will no longer provide a man shelter.

It was ghastly. The last words between us on the telephone. We cannot resolve things humanely. Where should we find such humaneness? Where does this idea come from, this idea that in the private sphere at least—and here again we separate the private from the societal—we ought to be able to solve problems in a humane manner?

Cutting the umbilical cord took a long time.

The couple structure proved to be a monolith, solid and impregnable. I wanted to rid myself, once and for all, of this obsession with being half a couple. This meant capturing one's own shadow, crawling into another skin, first shedding the old skin—it would not come off by itself.

The imprint seems indelible. To try to erase it one would have to counteract the brainwashing.

One would have to go through a period of withdrawal.

I have no peace of mind anymore. The entire fabric of love and passion and partnership, of sexuality and emotion and personal happiness, has become brittle right down to the last fiber. I stop thinking and living in terms of pairs—no matter which sex. Security, safety, and social acceptance crumble. I tear down my own dwelling in order to be free. It had been my home for many years. The wind already whistles through the slats, the wind of an unfamiliar emptiness, of a room where the game is played without rules, a room without old, without new people, a room sparsely populated by fabulous creatures who want to become new human beings.

Sometimes I become aware of something akin to sexual needs, occasionally an orgasm in my dreams. But if I think about whom to approach with these needs, I cannot decide. Do I have sexual needs? What are sexual needs? If they do exist, how can they be lived?

If a man is around, it is easier for woman to pretend that sexuality is livable in this society. Men have learned to channel their needs into genital activities, to satisfy them in quick coitus. Thus have they defined satisfaction. Women have played along. This has not undermined existing interpersonal relationships; it has instead strengthened them. The process of degeneration furthered. Penis and vagina are still called penis and vagina, and sexuality, because it continues to be a sphere detached from our lives, still goes under its own name.

Fenna is tearing at a paper napkin. It is evening and we are sitting on the terrace in front of the restaurant "Kastanie."

"Could you imagine loving a woman?" she asks and glances up.

"Yes," I answer and give a surprised laugh. "You, for instance!"
A chain of colored glass beads encircles her neck; she wears them

only in summer. I have to laugh again, amazed by this simple question and the ease with which I answered.

Fenna lays the shredded napkin aside. "Oh come on!" she says skeptically, summer lightning flashing through her eyes.

The woman we had been sitting with comes back from the telephone. We talk about other things. The sense of amazement persists. For the time being that is as far as it goes. We are not in love. We know only that we want to have something to *do* with each other. With this in mind the months pass into winter.

On the evening of my last day working in the hospital, the first thing I do is to banish the alarm clock from my room. From now on I will decide when to get up. I will get more than five hours sleep. My eyes will not be constantly inflamed. I am coming out of my slumber. My thoughts are turning cartwheels.

The autumn winds whip through our apartment. An invasion of catastrophes. The apartment is ready to burst. The first attempt at a new life is called off after less than a year. Three women with their men, no-longer-with-men, still-with-men, also-with-women, only-with-women, maternal impulses, and one child are faced with a heap of rubble. Yet another project come to naught at the hands of its initiators. In spite of all the plans proposals suggestions slogans, reality won out. What we had not reckoned with at all was a child and our misconceptions about caring for it.

To live for a woman and child! Have we reached a point where it is possible for a woman to live for a woman and child? Do I really want to take on the responsibility of a child I did not bear? Do I want to forgo being pregnant, giving birth, and nursing the child?

If I were to have a child, it would be with the full knowledge that I alone would be responsible for it. The experiences of people around me have made it clear that I cannot depend on anything or anyone aside from myself, whether on one man, one woman, a group of people.

I would have to sleep with a man in order to get pregnant. But I would not be capable of going to bed with a man merely for the sake of getting pregnant.

I would have to go back to work full-time in order to support the child. I would have to put it in a daycare center. If I had to work all day earning not much more than five hundred dollars a month—and then take care of the child in the evening—how could I find the time to grow?

My head was two steps ahead of my body. Our commune dissolved. In the city the apartment stands deserted. Not one of the three women really wants to take it upon herself to return and unearth what still lay buried in the rooms we left behind.

Hiding out. Three months. A transition.

Optimism should have been the driving force; new plans should have spurred me on. I was undecided and exhausted. This transitional period suited me fine. My room was tiny, but there was a window over my desk. It looked out onto a quiet courtyard; the sofa bed was a yard wide. Before going to sleep, I would put the cassette recorder right up next to the pillow so that I could listen to very soft music, one side of my face pressed up tightly against the silvery speaker.

The nights are my own again. Ideas come to me in the still of night, and I have time to pursue them. I have to be sure that no one will disturb me, that I won't meet anyone on the way to the kitchen or bathroom, that the telephone won't ring. At four in the morning I discover the sky. Dawn begins to rise from the edge of the world; the square of light stretched over the four-cornered courtyard grows azure and inflates to a dome. I lean out of the window. How can this pale strip of sky, which I usually notice only when I daydream or feel nostalgic, suddenly turn into an azure dome? My cheeks feel different. I'd like nothing better than to go down and build a fire by the garbage cans and play Rumpelstiltskin.

I can still feel in my bones all the mornings when I had to catch the train at a minute past seven and shortly thereafter start work in my stiffly starched uniform. Does the sky seem so blue just because I am the only one in the whole building who sees it at this time of day? It has been years since I found myself wide awake at four in the morning, energized by my own thoughts. Not on the weekend but in the middle of the week, not at a party, not with someone, but rather alone.

In the buried, bygone years I had been storing things up. Now that I am more alert, in a place with more time and more energy, I can finally piece together my fragmented thoughts.

I study the notes I have made over the past ten years and hesitantly begin to work my way through my past. The focal point of my existence has imperceptibly shifted to my own history and to the discovery of the woman I am now. It happens only rarely that I can write several days in a row. Outside demands are made on me. New groups, new projects, require my participation. Though in the back of my mind I ponder how I might better shield myself from too many demands, I nevertheless join in; this desire to take part is an almost automatic response. I make hasty decisions that turn out all wrong and that are followed by equally rash retractions.

New projects crumble faster than before; structures break down.

I wander back and forth between my exposed history and the dissolving structures surrounding me. I am thrown back on myself again and again. This is my nature. I am beginning to discover my capacity for change.

This has become the most important, most tangible, point of departure for everything that lies ahead.

I have planned a trip to America and Mexico. The time is right. Away from it all I will be able to get a better perspective, perhaps even make decisions. In any case, I will learn again what it is to travel.

For three months I have no visitors. Various women's groups meet occasionally in the living room of the apartment. I am not missing anything. But one night, sitting at my desk, I feel uptight. Behind me lie weeks of extreme exertion, weeks filled with preparations, projects, appointments. For the first time in nine months I made a date to meet a man for dinner. In fact, it is the first time in a long while that I spend an entire evening with someone. We talk for hours. We are unencumbered, new to each other. On the street we suddenly embrace, laugh. How simple it is, how automatic.

When I ruled out intercourse, other gestures that we had only as accessories to coitus were also precluded.

Access to women has been blocked off. When we try to find the way to our selves, our hands and feet are shackled. Do I find it more stimulating to appeal to a man than a woman? They have *broken our spirits*. This inadequate term, *socialization*! This prettifying concept, "conditioning."

We can move only if we move toward the opposite sex and even then only in the choreographed movements they taught us when they broke us to harness. We know how to act within these patterns, no matter how horrible the silence between the sexes may be, no matter how murderous the individual actions, how out of step or dissimilar the needs.

"No," I tell him. "I don't want you to touch me. I want to be able to touch Fenna in our own comfortable, natural way. I've known her longer than I've known you. I know her better than I know you. Why do I feel like I have so many arms and legs when I want to touch her?"

Between Fenna and me was the unspoken agreement that we didn't want to become involved with each other. If we had started making too many demands, had become preoccupied, had started longing for each other, our work would have suffered, and that we didn't want. Hours and hours in which we could paint and write would be lost, were we to really encounter and find out about each other.

But gradually it became impossible to ignore the changes that had taken place in us. It seemed as though I could almost reach out and grasp the affection that we sometimes felt for each other. When we met, we beamed at each other and blushed—without being able to turn our joy into a lasting embrace. I slept fitfully when we shared the same bed, afraid of getting too close to her in my sleep.

When walking, we put our arms around each other's shoulders or waist. Once in a while we stroked each other's hair. After women's meetings we parted with a sisterly embrace. We embraced with arms hands shoulders, cheek to cheek. Our lips met briefly in a fleeting kiss, and we laughed again and lightly ran a hand along the side of the other's face as if to indicate how much we would have liked to spend more time together.

We did not hug each other with breasts hips legs in these sisterly embraces. We did not kiss each other on the lips like leftist women and men so spontaneously force themselves to (sometimes it was even more likely that one would kiss the boyfriend of another woman than the woman herself).

We found ourselves in empty space. We didn't want to imitate; we wanted to create new ways and means of behavior drawing on our selves and on the untapped reserves of eroticism lying between us. The expanse of unexplored territory had a stupefying effect.

The memory of old behavior patterns faded ever so slowly. The transition seemed to be at hand.

State of Emergency

"It is easier for me to talk to women than to men," a woman friend tells me. "It is easier to live with women, easier to get along with them; I feel more comfortable around them than around men . . ."

"But why," I ask her. "Why do you have a relationship with a man, when it is easier for you to *talk, live,* and *get along* with women?"

"Approval, . . ." she says. "and it is . . . sexual. . . . I mean—I haven't had much experience with women, but maybe that was because it wasn't . . . any better than with a man . . ."

"I know what you mean," I say. "Fenna and I had problems too. Not because we wanted men's approval, but because we didn't know how to create a new, unique kind of passion—there is a kind of solidarity between women, one in which compassion, eroticism . . . sincerity and security are wrapped up together. Many of the feelings that often prove disastrous in relationships with men are at the same time . . . a reserve of strength which we can draw on for mutual support. Women's emotional resources are greater. With a man, emotional atrophy usually sets in so early that somewhere along the way he becomes incapable of having humane relationships . . . he can hold his own only as long as we are there to render him bodily and emotional . . . support . . ."

"But men are victims of conditioning, too!" she interrupts. "You can't blame them for . . ."

"I'm not!" I say. "I don't blame them for having learned that kind of destructive behavior expected of men . . . but, on the other hand, I *do* expect them to want to change—but I don't see any sign of that happening . . . not even with men who in terms of their work, life-style, intellect, would seem capable of changing, not even with men who claim that they would like to shed their masculine skin . . ."

"But they aren't all like that . . . sometimes it is possible to have . . . a humane relationship with a man . . . even sexually . . . a humane sexuality . . ."

"It is possible to have a humane sexual relationship with a woman," I counter.

"Even women try to control each other," she says. "Exclusivity has not been overcome; you still see jealousy, dramatic scenes, calamities . . ."

"It's such an easy way out to say that women haven't got all the answers either," I reply. "It goes back to the idea that women are supposed to be model human beings—simply because they are women . . . It is hard to be humane. When women get together, they are still just groups of human beings who have been deformed by society. They have certain basic things in common—their sex is the color of their skin. They share a common cultural, historical, sexist . . . past and still live in the same sexist society . . . among themselves they can cast off the traditional roles if they really want to—and here, it seems to me, the fundamental issue is one of a woman coming to terms with herself, whether or not she ever slept with another woman is not the important thing . . ."

"I agree," she says. "It is simply not true that it is necessarily better with women . . ."

"You're missing the point," I retort. "First of all it is a question of wanting to *fundamentally* change relationships between people, and this would imply, among other things . . . forgoing traditional relationships that are based on stereotypes. It is a question of woman realizing that she doesn't need another person to feel like a complete human being. But whether or not she will succeed depends upon the kind of work she does, her children, upon all the demands that are made on her—where can she find the strength to break free? The strength to become abnormal? To me it seems more and more unnatural, I really do mean *unnatural*, to have had access only to people of one sex. For the last twenty-six years, for example, I had to live without another woman's breast . . . how could I ever have known what it is like to bury my head in someone's breasts? When I am together with another woman I learn something about myself. With a man I learn only that I am different and that my body is supposed to be there for him, I don't really learn about my body or about myself . . ."

"But the electricity, the attraction . . . something is missing . . ."

"Do you mean that which is usually termed 'sexual arousal'?" I ask. "Doesn't anything happen when you're together with a woman? You don't feel anything in the pit of your stomach; you sit across from her, feeling a bit awkward perhaps . . ."

"Exactly," she says. "That's exactly how I feel!"

"Of course," I say, "but that's just it—then why do you still want to sleep with her? You feel this closeness to her, you have finally met up with that which you've always been giving to men, for the first time it is not only you who is paying attention, offering support and compassion, you are, instead, also the recipient, you sense another woman evoking in you a feeling of . . . longing, when up to now only men had found that women evoked feelings of longing in them . . . the man himself cannot evoke longing in you. Isn't it really the case that your sense of longing is the desire to evoke desire in him? . . . It isn't our body we learned to love . . . it is merely the desire that our body arouses in a man . . . do we love the male body or . . . do we love being desired? The period when the male body could evoke longings in us . . . belongs to the past—what is it you are really longing for when you long for that body?"

"But what about . . . approval? . . ." she says hesitantly. "Can you get along without men's approval?"

"What is it they should approve of? Is it important that they accept me, that in their eyes I conform to the image of what a woman should be? In fact, it's the eyes that really get to me, I mean literally these eyes that reflect the distorted bodies of women in rightist and leftist magazines. It is this distorted perspective . . . that we are supposed to measure up to, these eyes reduce me to an object . . . and, whether or not I feel whole, they dismember me, they focus on my breasts . . . this also happens with friends and acquaintances and not only with strangers on the street. I always get that uncomfortable feeling . . . that a man wants something from me. He invariably demands that I lavish my undivided attention on him as soon as he appears on the scene—because he is a man and I am a woman. He expects me to notice him, to be interested in him because he is a man and I am a woman—for no other reason! He naturally assumes that the woman who is graced with his approving stare is at his disposal. . . . I feel less inhibited among women . . ."

"But you are being just as one-sided," she says, "that's not any different . . ."

"But it is," I say, "it is different. I admit that it is one-sided, but that's not the issue, what is important to me is whether I am getting hurt, whether I am being weakened or strengthened . . . severed relationships can't be mended from one day to the next! . . . and why should women do that all by themselves? They provide the impetus; men have to take it from there. I cannot, for example, ignore the fact that, during all the thousands of years of male domination, the penis, just like all other implements . . . has become a weapon, and the attitude toward everything living has become correspondingly sadistic and destructive. The experiences most women have had with intercourse are ghastly enough without even mentioning abortions and torture."

"Everything has gotten so complicated!" she says. "But it must be possible to find one man somewhere with whom one could have a humane relationship. . . . I don't want to exclude him from my life, but I am no longer going to be there just for him alone; women are part of my life too . . ."

"I know, a man sometimes will sit there in the room without budging when he knows damn well that his woman wants to have a private conversation with other women!" We both start to laugh.

"This how-can-you-do-this-to-me look," she says, "because I am no longer there alone next to him! It didn't use to make any difference to him what I did—he had his work, his football buddies, his political group and me—but now that I have a women's group . . . what's going on with him? Sometimes a woman does arouse a new kind of feeling in me, a different kind of attraction . . . one that can, for a few seconds, be so intense that it carries over into the following day. It is also an erotic sensation, and it is fulfilling—it is not only the signal of some dubious need for 'more.' . . . I used to believe I was content all day after having slept with him, whether or not I had an orgasm, simply because I was with him—but now I feel empty when we sleep with each other, even though I do enjoy it, I do like having sex with him. . . . I do get aroused . . ."

"Do you really?" I ask, "or are you saying that only because the idea is so ingrained in your mind, and because you can rationalize intercourse that way? Don't we usually sleep with a man because of social pressures rather than because we . . . feel secure? Don't we often take a man in because that gives us the feeling of being needed. And if copulation is unpleasant or humiliating, we still have ample opportunity to remain somewhat detached—what goes on in the far reaches between penis and vagina doesn't really have to concern us. The penis is too . . . alien to be able to really reach us—this sort of schizophrenia has become incredibly complex and multifaceted! We need it for self-protection—in order to survive . . . we fake enjoyment in order to come up to expectations, in order to be left alone—can you talk to him about sexuality?"

"Hardly!" she says. "He gets scared, feels hurt, has guilt feelings—how am I supposed to tell him that I feel unfulfilled with sleeping with him . . . that I don't feel close to him, that weeks go by when I don't want to go to bed with him . . . perhaps things would improve if the intervals between intercourse were longer, if we would spend more time talking to each other. Can you talk to Fenna? Did you two have sexual problems?"

"Yes," I say. "It took a long time before we felt we could be open with each other, before we could talk about what each of us wanted. Even with her it took a long time before I believed that she actually found my body beautiful. It was, of course, different, hearing it from her than from a man, but I still didn't trust myself. . . . I noticed, too, that with a man the real sense of touch usually gets lost in the myriad of prescribed stimuli and responses . . ."

"Yes, that's how it seems to me, too. But how does this new way of touching become . . . different and yet exciting?"

"It takes time," I say. "Time played a really important role in building an intimate relationship. Now a new sense of longing, of excitement, of devotion has come into being—but it is devotion that stems from affection rather than from submission and brute force. This male society has gotten under our skin. It takes all the strength we can muster just to keep from perpetuating it, through conditioned gestures, wishes, activities, and reactions . . . why, for instance, do you put on makeup when you go out to meet a man, even though you don't wear any at home?"

"I want to look good, want him to find me attractive . . ."

"Do you go out to dinner with women, too? Do you find that exciting, fascinating; do you look forward to that, or does it seem less interesting than going out with a man? Don't women have anything to report about the big wide world out there; do you feel that only men, at least for a moment, can help you overcome the feeling of being closed in?"

"It is true that women's experiences out in the world are limited, but that isn't the problem. I'm more interested in women than in men; their history, their lives, are more interesting than men's; it's easier to talk to them. But when we are ready to leave . . . even if we walk home together . . . I just don't know where to go from there . . ."

*

The winter after my return from America is mild. In December we can go for walks in the gardens of the Charlottenburg Palace. Here and there crocuses are blooming. Fenna and I walk along with our coats unbuttoned. She stops, lifts her face toward the sun, and slowly says, I would like to be passionately in love again—I am not really interested in becoming involved, yet I'd like to experience that passion again, with a woman, I want to feel that special excitement as soon as I walk in the door. . . . I don't believe we are capable of that anymore.

I nod. Yes, I say, I feel the same way. But I still need time to recuperate. Recovering from the wounds inflicted over the past ten years is taking longer than I thought it would. I have no sexual needs. I want only peace and quiet, time to write. What do we really mean by passion, excitement?

A year ago, shortly before I left for America, the venture with Fenna began to take shape. We came upon regions of human affection which had lain fallow until then. We were not in love at the start, and we warily watched our moves. For a long time we were equipped with nothing but the knowledge that we wanted to have something to do with each other—we even had to learn how to speak. We were at one and the same time helpless and grateful in barren, unmapped territory.

> I am quite sure
> that you used to dwell in trees
> as I in lakes and rivers.
> In my glittering hair of moss
> solar energy erupted.
>
> Your strands of hair fanned down
> along the roots through the ground.
> They still store up memories
> of life within the mantle of bark
> each of the dark tendons
> is taut with the strength
> of survival in the forest. The gnarls
> on the trunks, these too
> you have brought along with you.
>
> Your hands coarse and damp
> the moment I want to live

with you, not just survive. An unreal
leafy green. You take
refuge in a corner of the blanket
to dry your hands, but also
to keep me out
of your life
and to hide so far away
that only the forest eyes can be seen and
the tiny roots of hair on your forehead.

Life in the water now long past
emerged
onto a barren rock. Surrounded by
perilous swamp, no end
in sight. The rock
no room for two
not yet enough ground broken
for a life outside the water
a bit of mossy hair,
in the sun.

You run lost through the woods, uprooted
hair, most women
long since expelled
or atrophied
crippled and brittle.
Only a few broke free
in time.

Many

   individually

         we hatch the world anew
         we stir up time
         we shed our shadow skin
         fire breaks out

I cannot remember anymore,

how many nights there were during that winter which is almost two years ago, nights when Fenna and I lay down together in the same bed — back to back — and warmed each other before curling up to sleep.

The matter-of-fact way in which we got undressed and crawled under the covers was comforting. Perhaps we murmured this or that to each other, lit a candle or two; when my feet got too cold I warmed them on her legs before we rolled over and snuggled up . . . we treated each other kindly and with great care. The weeks passed peacefully yet awkwardly. Since we did not know how to approach each other, we refrained from touching. Since we did not know how to view each other's bodies, we refrained from looking.

In the meantime I had become aware of my need to throw open my door after finishing my work and go to Fenna, placing one foot in front of the other as I went. A renewed desire to speak another language after work was done, a new language of skin words, laughing, bubbling, billowing sounds had surfaced within me.

I was treading water.

I could not think of any way to get things going between Fenna and me. The sincerity between us was so profound that I couldn't possibly be wily and underhanded. It seemed impossible to break down the reserve that Fenna had displayed when she helped me through my period of withdrawal from sexuality. It seemed that my intimacy with Nadjenka should have made it easier, but there was no comparison. Nadjenka and I were cut from much the same cloth. It was not difficult for us to touch each other. We soon found that we shared a common need, and we could immerse ourselves in it. This was the way it had always been for me. If I didn't feel a certain immediate inexplicable attraction toward the other person, I couldn't make love happen.

This time, though, eroticism developed only gradually. Hesitantly, timorously, it dissipated as soon as we drew back from each other. It lacked vital energy at first.

But there was at least this sense of having the reins in one's own hand for the first time, of not being drawn into a preconceived pattern, of not being led by incomprehensible series of actions and reactions. One had the sense of spinning the threads of one's own fate wittingly.

From time to time we spent a whole day together taking long walks. It was on one of those occasions that we went to Fenna's house afterward to listen to music. Sitting there, we cuddled up to each other. Our eyes met in agreement; our faces began to draw closer and stopped just before touching. I could submerge myself in the shadowy crescents beneath her eyes. The rim of her iris glimmered green in the last few rays of sun streaming through the window panes. The green emitted light gray beams flecked with amber which converged upon the pupil. The smiling lashes descended slowly and interlaced with those below.

We could hardly draw apart, sighing, laughing, "why haven't we ever . . ."—the obstacles seemed to have been overcome. But as time went on they imposed themselves between us again and again.

Although we went away shortly thereafter and spent a whole week together on a farm, we did not go to bed with each other.

Only the nocturnal hours could have brought us closer, since we were not alone. Besides, Fenna needed the daylight hours for painting. We wanted to make use of the time and peace and quiet, and we did not want to neglect our work in favor of sexuality.

Was that really it?

Wasn't it really the fear of losing one's head, the possibility of our lives becoming too entangled, the uncertainty about whether we were indeed capable of remaining individuals while carrying so much of each other within us?

We vacillated because we had both grown used to being alone, we knew that, in some ways at least, it was simpler to face problems alone.

Piece by piece, dear sister
life by life
fossil by fossil
history by history
fingertip by fingertip
approach by approach
smile by smile
word upon word
skin upon skin
affection upon affection
Oh, sister dear
You'll be amazed at what mountains we build!

Strange things happened that week on the farm. On top of all the difficulties we created for ourselves, there were also external circumstances that kept us from getting together. It did not take much to keep us at a distance.

Just after our lips had taken up from where our last kiss had ended, we were interrupted by cats yowling beneath our window. Our hearts stopped beating; we sat bolt upright in bed. Wasn't that the shadow of a man? Was it really just the wind rustling through the trees? Sobered and wide awake, we lay next to each other, apart once again.

"Cats," murmured Fenna, drifting off to sleep, "it would have to be cats that disturb us!"

Another night, as we embraced in spite of suffering from sunburn and chills, we heard a strange, scratching sound behind us: a tiny mouse was sitting on the pillow. One leap, and we were both standing in the middle of the room. The mouse disappeared into a hidden crevice. We lay down again and agreed that, though we weren't really afraid of mice, we didn't especially like for one to crawl over us. I could not sleep. I kept hearing the scratching every so often, at four in the morning I actually found the mouse sitting next to my head again.

A group of us women had gone together to a vacation spot at the ocean. The castle we were living in was huge, a labyrinthine building with many entranceways.

In the village there was a small old bathhouse, a relic of bygone days. It even had a sauna. We had arranged to meet the old village woman there. Fenna planned to make love to her with all of us there looking on. It was a ritual; no one thought it strange.

The old one was wizened and withered and clothed all in rags. One almost expected her to reek of cod liver oil. She hobbled about in shoes made of animal skins. She spoke not a word but was very friendly, serene; she had made her peace with the world.

We sat there in the bathhouse and waited for her to arrive. After she came in, she sat down on the floor and began to take off her stockings, very slowly and ceremoniously. I was sitting next to her. Her heavy gray cotton stockings covered enormously hefty legs bulging with varicose veins. We were awed by her ugliness, for we knew that this was what awaited women at the end of their lives. We wanted to rid ourselves of the aesthetic prejudices we still carried within us, wanted to begin to revere the ancient misshapen old ones like her.

It all took too long to suit me; I left. Later on, the others told me that the ritual had not taken place after all—why, I don't know.

How could Fenna and I overcome our shyness and fear? How were we to learn to touch, kiss, confront the lips between our legs?

Is it this image that shocks people into reacting so defensively when the subject of lesbian love is broached? One allows one's own hand, a man's hand, a penis, a man's mouth, to do that which is forbidden between women.

We have learned to kiss the penis, and yet are afraid of the
lips between our own legs.
The hand on its way to the clitoris
of another woman
traverses centuries.
It can get lost a thousand times.
It fights its way through fragments of civilization.
And in addition, the route it takes
leads to a place that has no name:
I have no clitoris.
I have no vagina. No vulva. No pussy.
No bust, no nipples.

My body is corporeal. There are no places on my body which correspond to these incorporeal and brutal designations. Clitoris has nothing in common with this part of my body which is called clitoris. In order to find new words I will have to live differently for as many years as I have lived believing in the meaning of these terms.

This part of my body which is called clitoris is not my focal point; my life does not revolve around it. It is not that I want to minimize its importance; it is just that I do not want to be limited again to only one part of my body.

I am beginning to see myself for what I really am.

I assemble the separate parts to make one whole body. I have breasts and a pelvis.

My legs run together to form curves, folds, lips. I glide and fall with Fenna through meadows of blossoming labella (only a man could have named one of these erotic feminine flowers *snapdragon*).

From now on we'll just call them vulva-flowers, Fenna decides.

I set the scene: Hello, I'd like a
                   bunch of vulva-flowers . . .
What do you want? Get out of here!
Fenna and I convulse with laughter.

That's not right, I interrupt; having a vulva is nothing to be ashamed of. I take a good look at myself, become immersed in the hues, the shadings, the variegations of skin. The lips of my vulva are wrinkled folds. They really do look like rolled-up flower petals, reddish-brown and bright pink when I gently unfurl them. How many different unknown shades of colors to be discovered on my body! We create ourselves anew by touching, looking, talking. My breasts pendulate before her body; they begin to laugh, to vibrate with novel sensations. Gently I place a breast on her eye. How apropos that in German men say, "It fits like a fist in the eye" . . .

 —It looks nice

Um hm, purplish—
 —Couldn't you go on any longer?

No, I'd lost you—
 —Yeah, it really is difficult sometimes . . .

Bubbles of laughter fill the room. Genital solemnity, where is your sting?

"I still can't quite deal with our relationship," said Fenna in the last conversation before I left for America. "I can't fit us into my life. I don't even know whether I want to—my painting is still the most important thing to me." I felt rejected. "What we have between us hasn't helped me up to now. I am still afraid of being taken over," she went on.

She was sitting way over on the other side of the bed. I reached over my hand, an emissary.

"Don't," she said. "Don't touch me. I have to talk first."

"We can talk and touch," I countered.

She refused. "I can't do both."

The initial difficulties we encountered in linking one life to the other surfaced again and again. They did not seem to diminish as time passed. They were still able to overpower us. We constantly expressed our doubts about whether or not we even wanted to let another person become so important to us. We felt too threatened by the possibility that our feelings would lead to uncontrollable passion, pain, peril. Where does one draw that thin line between seeing each other only seldom and remaining total strangers, between intimacy and addiction? Our encounters were few and far between. There always seemed so little for us to build upon. Our trust in each other did not seem to be increasing, nor did our reticence readily wane. At each encounter it took a while to reestablish our ties.

Talking still exhausted me. It was hard labor for me to learn to speak. After two hours I was totally worn out.

We could never take refuge in sexuality; for us it could never serve as a substitute language for things left unsaid, undone; it could never be used to camouflage problems. Being together demanded a great deal of time. Our intimacies were circumspect. In the time it took for us to exchange a single kiss, I would in the past have already had intercourse and found myself standing there fully clothed and ready to depart.

Today I am leaving for America, I said to myself the following morning, as I wandered home through the empty streets. I had to laugh. The word *America* did not mean anything to me. I knew only that I would be away for three months. There was nothing left for me to do in Berlin, nor was I looking to find anything. It was enough to glide naked through space for a time, covered only by Fenna's warm dry lizard skin.

In Frankfurt I made one last call to Nadjenka. Her voice still echoed in my ears long after I had arrived in New York.

I am worried about you, she says.

Wanting to reassure her, I say, Nothing is going to happen to me.

I always worry about you, she says, you don't need to go to America for that.

I had not seen her for a long time. I saw her at a women's conference in spring, but we didn't really have a chance to talk. She had driven in with a friend in order to see me. But I was all involved in special meetings. She caught me on the run between workshops, plenary sessions, and discussions with other women, I was terribly busy, I was all wrapped up, I had no time to sit down and have a private chat with her. Politics was the issue of the moment.

Could our conference have any meaning for Nadjenka, any impact on her, on her daughter, her husband, her household, her life in the suburbs?

I felt a pang when I saw her. Why didn't we have any projects in common? Was my work with these women really irrelevant to her life? Why didn't *she* undertake anything? She attempted to laugh on the wing. Her fair hair still fluttered about her face. She stood there next to the woman she had come with, who also had a child. They seemed able to give each other mutual support; they were thinking of going on vacation together.

Her life is changing, I thought.

She will get along without me.

When had I ever offered her help?

Would it really have helped if I had shared my life with her?

I was not willing to take the risk of restructuring my own life, of beginning a new life with her. We had only talked about *her* venturing the new beginning, the leap into the unknown, the break with the past; she was supposed to be the one to finally pull herself together and raze her former dwelling . . . at that time I had not realized how much I was asking of her. I only saw how uncomplicated my life was in Berlin, how easy it was to make contact with the many groups, I was young, I had time, time enough to ask Nadjenka to come and join me in Berlin.

She felt old and all worn out, thirty, feared the unknown . . . the leftists didn't impress her. How could I, myself a ghetto dweller, have countered her objections? She watched me moving from one commune to the next, running through group after group, humanizing man after man.

Seeing you again at the women's conference was very painful for me, wrote Nadjenka. I got the feeling that we didn't really mean that much to each other anymore, that our relationship had lost that special something. Something had come between us. You parcel out your affection equally to everybody—I get my share too, of course, but there is nothing special about it.

Her voice reaches me through the telephone: I'm worried about losing you.

Don't be ridiculous, Nadjenka, how could that possibly happen?

Another woman could make it happen, she says. Only another woman can come between us. I was never afraid of losing you before; a man was never a threat to what we had.

Not even another woman could break up our relationship, I say. It isn't Fenna that you fear; it is the strength I draw from the women's movement, my close ties to those women, the importance I attach to my work with women. . . . I do relate to you differently now than I used to when on the rebound from a man . . . but that doesn't mean that you're not still someone very special to me—no, I repeat, it isn't Fenna. It is that your life is so different from mine while Fenna's and mine are so alike—both of us are single, neither of us has children, we're both involved with Bread ♀ Roses . . . for more than two years we have been helping shape that group and give it new direction.

For months Nadjenka kept me at arm's length; nothing changed until she came to visit me at the beginning of the following year. She didn't want me to be a part of her life anymore; she shut me out only to take me back in again; she weighed the situation, pondered. She tried to examine the strands of her life, tried to untangle those hard knotted strands. I didn't hear from her all the while I was gone; she doggedly remained silent.

"There were times when I really missed you while you were in America," said Fenna, as we walked through the gardens of the Charlottenburg Palace. "I can't tell you exactly what it was, but it seemed to be more difficult to cope with things. Conflicts were harder to resolve; once when I had my period I just broke down—not that I necessarily wanted to spend more time with you, it was more . . . the idea that I could discuss my problems with you. . . . I longed for your . . . emotional support."

The summer had passed us by. The warmth would have favored our attempts to get together, I thought. Now we will have to bundle ourselves up again in two or three layers of clothes, coats caps scarves and gloves.

Brussels, a telephone booth. My head spinning, the first thing I did upon arriving was to change some money.

Hello? Fenna's voice on the other end.

It's me, I finally say.

Veruschka! Where are you?

In Brussels.

If I leave right away, she says slowly, I can meet you in Frankfurt, and we can still drive back tonight.

I steady myself on the wall of the phone booth. You mean you're really going to come pick me up?

She laughs. What do you think I meant?

"This bond between us, . . ." I said, as we continued our walk through the gardens, "I think it has something to do with that nebulous notion of 'motherliness.' That term is so ambivalent, so ambiguous . . . how can we attain immediate, direct access to motherliness? For too long we have been thought of as nothing but furrows for sowing seeds—the issue here isn't . . . the woman who gave birth to each of us . . . it's not the blood ties, the guilt feelings, the silence that we want; it . . . isn't a question of making amends, of motherliness only toward her; the issue is the power of motherliness, motherliness as a shared human characteristic . . ."

Two days before Easter it is snowing, sodden, and ugly. When I had taken a walk in the park at Christmas, the forsythia were blooming.

I curse as I put on my heavy winter coat, hurry to the subway, and immerse myself in a book. I'm *already* snowed in, lost to the world. Last night I was taught to swim like a fish, to cleave through the waters, to part the seas, to furrow them. Mightier than the oceans!

After treating my private patient, I return to the apartment, swearing a blue streak. Some nice soup will come to my rescue; you can always depend on cauliflower. I wash the dishes in order to warm my hands. I would like nothing better than to refill the sink with fresh hot water for each and every dish.

My head, charged with bolts of lightning from the ride on the subway, is ready to burst. The soup is steaming next to the typewriter; it tastes like cardboard and like the gray walls in front of my window, its warmth only skin deep. Soon there will be ice water flowing through my veins. I take refuge in the kitchen, turn on all three gas burners, and let the blue flames flare; I want to put on some water for tea, pour it into me by the gallon until I am thawed out. I let the laundry run through the machine two, three, five, ten times, hotter than blazes!

The washing machine is sizzling, the plastic is melting, the kitchen is steaming, my hair is standing on end, my head explodes. Cold sweat, with clammy fingers I turn off the gas flames, the washing machine.

I'm getting my period.

The uterus lies cramped between the pelvic bones. The lining of the inner walls is saturated with blood. Dark brown spots for three days now, traces of bright red on the tampon. The lining stubbornly refuses to detach itself. It is taking unusually long this time; it's a nuisance. My head is spinning, and this waiting weighs upon me like oppressive weather. The skin on my abdomen is more taut than usual, stretched tightly over the contracting uterus, the pelvic musculature has become too tense, it tugs downward. In previous months the pain had been sudden and acute. Almost the whole lining had been expelled the first day, dark clots. But immediate relief had followed, my tummy warm and relaxed, a premonition of what a period could be like.

Nadjenka came to see me. It can only have been two weeks ago, yet it seems as if she has been gone forever. The long weekend was much too short; afterward I was filled with an emptiness as never before; I could hardly warm up again. At night her life preyed upon me, tore at my breast.

The pain radiating, sometimes I have to stop in my tracks. To have your period on the weekend, of all times, the two days without interruption from the outside world. Monday is shot—private patients in the morning and the afternoon spent at the clinic where I work part-time. Just looking at the typewriter gives me a backache. (My back is killing me, says a patient, I have the curse.) The muscles contract again and again in order to loosen the lining. Nadjenka's spasmodic sobs still cling to me; she is choking; her life is strangling her. I rock her gently, tell me what's wrong . . .

Never had a choice. Became a secretary because there was no money for anything else, married to get away from home, to finally have a home, had a child, after many years finally a child, in order to . . .

"What'll happen to you, if anything happens to her?"

Nadjenka becomes faceless. Impossible to imagine. "It's simple," she says then, slowly. "Either I'll go on living without her or I won't."

"Perhaps."

What a burden for a mother to bear, right from the very moment of conception, this anticipation of being abandoned. Is life to be reduced to the attempt to overcome loneliness?

"Berlin wouldn't have been the answer, I know that for sure now," she says. "I needed someone to take me by the hand, and you couldn't have done that. You can't imagine the shape I would have been in, how dependent I would have been on you, at least for quite some time."

Each of us had had a man at our side at that time; later our lives took decidedly different courses. Perhaps our getting together would have destroyed everything?

She is my alter ego. When I encounter her, I encounter a part of myself as well. No shared projects, outside interests, hardly a common history. Yet the intimacy lingers, no matter how seldom we see each other. If we were together, would we discover that much was lacking? Is this intimacy really a basis, or is it ultimately only that which we cannot—or only with great difficulty—achieve with other people? Someone approaches me the same way I approach others—does that make her my alter ego, is Nadjenka a mirror image, or are we mistaken, but, if so, about what . . . why shouldn't we believe each other, why shouldn't we be able to shelter each other, be close to each other despite spatial distance?

Perhaps my period is all loused up this time; maybe everything is blocked up. I get the speculum and take a look. The mouth of the cervix appears from the depths, stands out glistening, brilliant between the coral walls enclosing it.

Out of the circular opening a drop of bright red blood, more of them gather, run down from the vault of the cervix, the confluence of the red river. I can't help smiling; the flashlight illuminates more than the cervix. The darkness of the past fifteen years pales. For fifteen years, every month, red days. I have *my* period; it belongs to me. Having my period was my only chance to belong to myself.

I remember back to the days in school when the girls who were menstruating had to bring a note from their mothers to be excused from gym. Each girl was terribly proud the first time she could present this note: it made her a member of the secret society; it gave her a certain feeling of power. Once in awhile, just for the fun of it, all of us would appear before the gym teacher with forged excuses; disconcerted, he would mutter: But—you can't—all—at the same time . . . how could he prove the contrary? So we were free to leave; as soon as he came, we took off. Menstruation was a collective event. The cramps, clenched teeth during class, fleeting conversations in the bathroom—all of that met with an understanding smile, a knowing glance.

The traces on the tampon are bright red for one more day. But then the cramps grow stronger, they radiate out from the uterus; I get diarrhea. I lie down, toss and turn trying in vain to find a comfortable position. The warmth from the heating pad finally seems to help a bit; I drink hot tea with milk. It still hurts; I curl up into a ball, anything to keep from having to straighten my back now. The blood is rushing through my head as usual, I am sweating; all at once saliva collects in my mouth, and I try to fight it off but finally stumble to the toilet and spit up the tea. My face is blotchy and contorted. I lie down again; it seems to have passed. Another day is ruined; perhaps by evening I'll be able to think clearly again.

State of Emergency

A woman travels through Germany
ten bleak hours through the chill of night.
Already at the signal of departure
her face shatters
penned in among the sultry vapors of the moving train

she rebels
to avoid being crushed by that fragment of life
at her disposal

Myself outside
before the icy window pane
my breasts sway
anxiously to and fro
a long night coming as the train rushes on
from the fibers of my lips
grow incredulous blossoms

into her abandonment. How far removed
from me she rests
with the deep folds between her legs
from which she brought forth
a daughter, to avoid remaining
alone in that fragment of life
at her disposal.

At the first light of dawn
my anxious breasts must yield.
Lost blossoms wander to and fro
unfathomable between us
to and fro.

Now the red stream is flowing strong: one tampon can dam it for no more than two hours. My breasts don't hurt anymore, but the web of veins is bluer than usual. I am restless, overwrought, I sleep fitfully, am worn out when I get up; by hand I write words and lines that I constantly rearrange. In the afternoon I get tired and try to sleep for an hour. The merry-go-round inside my head keeps me cold and tense; my body remains suspended an inch above the bed; only gradually does it yield; sinking, the pillow meets me halfway; I can finally rest my head. The cries of the children playing in the yard fade away; their ball rolls out of earshot. My toes make my stockings cold. I glide into darker interstages; the walls of the room disappear. My racing heartbeat brings me back; I bury my head in the sleep-enticing folds of the pillow, but it's no use.

At night I walk with other women along a southern coast. The cliff drops sharply to the dark-blue, turquoise-mottled sea below. We have to fight our way against a wall of wind, but, while the others move on forward, I am caught up in a funneling draft of air and slung in spirals toward the sky. Flying! I spread my arms. Above me an incandescent seagull floating with me in the same ethereal stream. In gentle waves we glide through the luminous heavens.

This year I had enough time to spend five weeks in the north of Germany. My need for space, for room to breathe, was satisfied in a new way; space gave way to other space. The unsettling vastness of faraway places, the disquieting expanse of foreign lands, the stimulating space of the cities – all these needs were not yet satisfied, yet I did not long for those other places.

Vastness

in which the sun still shone brightly, pouring its balmy light across the sky. The yarrow growing wild at the bottom of the field was so high that I disappeared in it whenever I waded toward the fence to gaze across the meadow. High above in the blue streaked with white, an airplane left its trail every evening at the same time. Oddly enough, I didn't sense the usual pang of take-me-along.

Sitting there behind the house and watching the sinking sun, I began to remember that about two years ago this longing for trees, sky, space, had last surfaced in me. But since then I hadn't been aware of it, or, if it had arisen for a moment, I hadn't taken it seriously. It was two years ago, when returning from a trip to Switzerland after spring vacation and landing at the airport in Berlin, that I noticed that the exhilaration of being home was missing. That hadn't happened in five years. Even on the long bus ride home, the usual excitement of being home again was absent. I knew where I was, swayed nonchalantly past familiar buildings and shop windows. I must be exhausted, I decided. I have to get up at six tomorrow; there won't be any time to think until the weekend.

When I reached the apartment I was sharing with the other women, I landed right in the middle of a group meeting. I felt a strong sense of aversion. The naked bulb hanging down in the living room burned brightly, inhospitable as always; I could only make out the silhouettes of the various women. I wanted peace and quiet, wanted to be home at last. Something was pulsating in my head, dark green shadows. The floodwaters of the Aare River, which had impressed me so, rose inside me for a moment as I put down my bags in my dark room. The walks along the lush overgrown banks, pleasantly light and sunny—I'd done nothing but take walks and look around.

Hours later, when I slipped between the smooth sheets, the green shadows of the darkness began to grow; they overran my bed; a rustling filled the room: there were forests, whole forest regions reflected in the train windows from Bern to Zurich.

I'm getting old, I thought to myself that night on the farm, as I drifted off to sleep. At least the landscape of Switzerland doesn't disturb me anymore.

I am a slow brooder. I walk around for days without finding any words, or can't choose between the words I do find. They are all inadequate. It wouldn't be so bad if all I had to do was choose the words and then arrange them in a certain order, construct the phrases and arrange them in a certain pattern, and, having done this, find that everything I wanted to say would be there in black and white. But I must create new words, must be selective, write differently, use concepts in a different way. Every so often a word breaks out of my walled-in brain. In the morning I often awaken in the middle of a sentence, at night, agitated, I jump out of my warm nest, a word, an image, paper, pencil! Quick, before the landslide in my head begins, before I can clack away at the typewriter until my arms fall off. I let them lie there. The skin on my forehead is cool from the beads of icy sweat. I am full and empty.

There is lightning in the courtyard. The stagnant heat has paralyzed me for days. With arms folded I stand at my window. If only it would start to pour. The bleak light tries to peel away the heat from the walls of the building, but it tenaciously refuses to yield. Across the adjoining parking lot bits of paper whirl about in the breeze. An arid wind begins to blow between the buildings, the gusts becoming stronger and stronger.

The light reminds me of the fallow horses Fenna and I had once seen in the country, the tiny foals nestling up against the bellies of the mares.

A door slams shut. I leave the window and walk through the almost empty apartment. Three of the women have gone on vacation. The wind has already scattered the papers lying about on their desks. Will I be able to breathe more freely in this apartment after the storm has blown over? Ever since I came back from the farm it has seemed stifling and cramped in here.

"I figured you would probably come back feeling somewhat alienated and out of touch," said a woman I live with.

I close the windows. The high ceilings, the walls, everything is closing in on me. I feel like a mummy in this setting. I'd like to empty all six rooms with one fell swoop, throw open all the doors and windows. How could I ever have thought this apartment so large? I take all the pictures down from the walls of my room. Fenna brings me her painted clouds of the north German sky.

The light has turned sulfureous. The room grows dim; the wind has done its job. Now the rain begins to trickle down.

I stretch my hands out of the window. How they were filled with Fenna's full lush lips. They floated through my fingers. My hands a chalice, I search for imprints left behind, but only a calyx of fragrance remains.

Just now in the bathroom
I wanted to take a cold shower because I
felt faint
I noticed that I still
am a bit tan at least
the skin tone on my shoulders and neck
is different than
where my breasts begin
Fenna! and I write you a letter since I wonder
when you'll ever have the time and chance
to observe,
at length and in detail
as such observation demands, that
the skin tone on my shoulders and neck
is different than
where my breasts begin?

We constantly
come up against
limits in our explorations. The limits
of our own strength of available time of
economic resources, of our careers and
our longings. When can we
clarify what longings really are? How can we make
room for our sensual life? The new
emerges but slowly, shedding the old, patchwork.

Do you know this feeling in your abdomen

when the uterus for no apparent reason
contracts and sensations arise out of
fear of being tested, out of sexual desire and
menstrual pain? For years this feeling has now and
again surfaced even when I was under no
extraordinary pressures in the middle of the day
perhaps without apparent cause.

But if I think of
how I felt in the kitchen as a child,
I can retrace the faint trail—
relationships which have been severed
or damaged beyond repair.

Last night in my dreams I stood before a three-paneled mirror.
When I looked straight in, I saw my face as it looks back at me during
the day or in recent photos; only my hair was still long and piled atop
my head. When I turned my head to the left, my face changed in that
side of the mirror; it was my eyes that were first transformed. Bruises
appeared all around my eyes, dark blue on my eyelids purplish along
my cheekbones. My eyebrows became bushy and black my skin
wilted. My hair turned gray and coarse.
     It did not surprise me that my face had aged.
     But it became the face of a total stranger. Not a single line was
familiar. If I turned straight ahead again, I saw my real face. So the
old woman in the left half of the mirror must have something to do
with me. I was startled because the face seemed disfigured, and I
moved closer to get a better look at the bruises. I discovered a delicate
pattern of veins in the purplish marks. I turned sideways to the left
portion of the mirror and looked at my shoulders then my back. A
shawl was draped across my shoulders: a veil of twining tendrils and
flowers green blue and red. From above the aged face peered down at
me. Fenna, I said, look, look how beautiful that is!
What's going on here? My face ages on my
body a new fabric. I finally realize
that I always thought my body unfashionable
out-of-date, and that thinking it
out-of-date actually spared me much.
If I hadn't complicated matters so much
carrying my body around a dead weight,
if I hadn't lugged it around as I did

I would have been more completely co-opted by
everyday sexuality. My body itself kept that from
happening. It didn't measure up to
male expectations.
I can recognize fragments of my own past history
as well as that of all other women.
There is a trend that gives direction
to the future even in the present
there are multiple layers of processes going on at
different speeds rhythms and on
different levels.
There is no simultaneity to be found. The various
processes collide inside of me
at different points in time with varying degrees
of impact—this sense that life is sometimes
so *compacted*. Even though it is already a
thing of the past I often think of
what I felt on the flight back from New York.
I knelt on the floor and pressed my face against
the window as the plane took off. Far below
the coast disappeared, a white outline. When I
saw that it actually resembled the one
on the globe I had a fleeting image of
America and an idea of the contours of the globe
as a whole. Again I felt this urgent desire to
know the *world* as I flew back to Europe, back to
Berlin without knowing what I was still seeking there.
But in these last glimpses of the American coastline
I had a certain feeling, one that flared up only to
die down again, a feeling that I was not really
returning but rather moving on without ever
taking hold.
How casually this giant continent
coasts into the ocean!
It gave me such a lift, seemed so simple and
natural seeing it, the confines of my own body
could expand for a few moments.
Our being, on the other hand, is
boxed in on all sides.
Now that it seems that we are not smothering
each other even though the intimacy has grown

now that the perils of a love affair
while not completely ruled out
have so far at least been held in check . . .
now we notice that we can't do anything right.
A long time ago
we began with the vague desire
to have something to *do* with each other. Now that
it is really a serious matter, we find there are
so many obstacles to overcome. We must constantly
neglect something in favor of something else.
The job suffers because of political activities the
political activities because of the job
the job on the other hand doesn't bring in
enough money earning money takes time away from
our other important work.
We lose each other along the way. Constantly having
to decide
between us and our work—that too a
conflict—if we neglected our work the perils
of a love affair would mount. Painting and
writing to some extent offer tangible guidelines,
it is only because of these that we can survive,
that we can attempt to transcend
the tragically restrictive means of communication
open to us.
But we cannot rise above the fits of anger and
despair.
Tomorrow morning I will ring your doorbell you
will open the latch I will drop these pages into
your mailbox, having compressed into a few lines
that which would require many hours
not perhaps to capture
our longings but to communicate them
not perhaps to live but to suspend
merely surviving
for a few hours.

Gourd Woman

It was already a little after eight-thirty.

Cloe got up in a daze. As she ran down the long hall to the telephone, her breasts ached; she cradled them protectively in her hands. When she sat down and picked up the receiver, she felt a twinge in her ovaries. Had another four weeks gone by?

Six or seven periods ago her breasts had started hurting a few days before menstruation, especially when she ran. Ever since she had begun loving her breasts, life had come into them, hence, pain as well.

After finishing the conversation she put the receiver back on the hook and walked slowly into the bathroom. When she looked up into the mirror, still bending over the washbasin, shaking the water from her face and reaching for the towel, she couldn't help but smile. In the mirror two soft pale brown gourds nodded toward the basin. In the country sunshine fine white hairs had become visible. Cloe laughed aloud. Porcupine breasts! she murmured. Gourd-porcupine, porcupine-gourd. . . . She thought of the forbidden oval and round shapes. The womb, a ripened gourd, entrance to the vault, dwelling of the mouth of the womb, an oval shape . . .

She had slept poorly.

These past weeks she'd been totally out of touch. She didn't know whether to look first to the right or to the left when crossing the street; she would stand on the corner until the green light finally turned red and only then start across. Twice already it had happened that she couldn't unlock the door to the building at night because she had been turning the key the wrong way. If footsteps approached her room, she would draw her shoulder blades together in fright and hold her breath—hoping no one wanted to come in. It was almost impossible for her to walk through the living room if someone was sitting in there. She felt hemmed in by expectations of a glance, recognition, a conversation.

She listened to music when she needed to take a break from writing. She was no longer capable of relating to anyone during these intervals. Sometimes she would have liked nothing better than to sit down on the kitchen floor in front of the washing machine and spend hours staring at the colored laundry that tumbled to and fro.

Cloe turned off the water and plunged her face into the towel. The skin on her face was beginning to get bumpy again; it had started on the way back from the farm. Along her lower jaw, just in front of her ear, a white spot had suddenly erupted and begun to itch and swell.—Nono, I'm sure nothing stung me, this just happens sometimes. Now they had started appearing one after the other in the course of the day; occasionally a new one would be there when she woke up. From time to time the skin would prickle all over her body, grow taut, stretched too tightly around her, protesting against clothing, noise, dirt, sweat, and confrontations with people. Sometimes Cloe's skin would not relax until, naked, she slid between the covers and turned off the lights. She was worn and frazzled to the breaking point. She fervently envied people who could lie down *and fall asleep*. Most of all she envied people who could lie down to sleep *because* or *when* they were exhausted. Were she to lie down now, her eyelids would refuse to grow heavy. She would circle behind them, a bundle of gray fluff trying in vain to sink into the listless somnolent expanse above which she floated.

She put on her long dress and, in someone else's slippers that were too large for her, shuffled into the kitchen to heat water for tea. Then she fished the turquoise-colored mug out of the dirty dishes and began to wash it. What urgent little details *life* consists of! The shawl of morning sunlight about her shoulders almost seemed more than she deserved. Hadn't she yet learned to accept what was her due?

Cloe put her hands down; the warm water from the faucet kept flowing over her hands. The scrub brush slid out of one hand; the mug dangled from the other. Lost in thought, she gazed out the window. Warmth suddenly seemed to be the most important thing in life. The warmth of the sun.

From now on I will think in light-years, she said aloud, and then quickly looked around, startled. But she was alone in the kitchen. Today was one of those days when layers of dreams, fragments of conversations that she'd had or read somewhere, half-forgotten encounters, all hovered in the air like particles of soot after a great fire.

Cloe scrubbed the mug vigorously and set it on the table. I have to clarify where I'm *at,* she thought. No, first I have to figure out *how I got to* this point. I don't know how all these things get into my head. Ever since I've been working and living differently, thoughts and images have been crowding my mind. Not only do I need to get this stuff out of my head, I also have to recollect when and how it got in there, and it is precisely *that* which cannot be put into words. By the time the impressions and thoughts are roaming around inside me, and I have started wondering how they entered my mind, they are already distorted. I must guide them into my head so that I can express them in familiar signs, so that others will be able to understand them. These numerous processes of assimilation and alienation must evolve in such a way that the signals emerging from my head and going into the typewriter correspond as closely as possible to the *original* experience, though in another form . . .

The water was boiling. Whenever Cloe showed something she had written to anyone it was already obsolete by the time she got around to discussing it. The words and their sequence were constantly changing in her head. She had to put a stop to that. She didn't believe the claim that a book was "finished" only when each printed sentence could be expressed in one way and no other. A book a process a piece of life, Cloe said to herself—all *change*able.

She took the box of tea down from the shelf, shook a handful of black leaves into the tea strainer, poured some boiling water over it, and let the tea steep for a few moments. As she held the tea kettle with her right hand waiting to pour the rest of the water into the pot, she again felt the piercing pressure on the inner edge of her shoulder blade. Sometimes while driving she had hardly been able to lift her arm when she wanted to turn on the radio. Unpleasant sensations radiated from this spot, as though all the muscles, sinews, and nerves above and below the shoulder blade were twisted and sprained.

Lately it seemed so senseless to discuss the book with anyone. People's comments only added more rings of emptiness to the ones already encircling her. Her narrative sources had grown silent.

Lately there came hardly a clue from the things she was working on; even from the letters themselves there emanated an unsuspected coldness now and then. Frozen solid they surrounded her.

Cloe lifted the strainer out of the pot and emptied it into the garbage bag. She poured herself some tea, sat down at the table, and warmed her hands around the steaming mug. I think I'll dye my hair today, she decided. It was consoling to think of the greenish goo working by itself while she pored over the manuscript, so that after two hours her hair would shimmer reddish gold. A year ago she'd had her hair clipped very short. She had wanted to see the shape of her head again and the contours of her face – and she had hoped that with short hair she would not be accosted on the street as often. Her hair had grown in quickly, stronger and fuller. She already had to brush it out of her eyes. She imagined the woman she had been a year ago and the woman the year before that and . . .

Shedding.

This is the year of the gourd woman! She got up and went into her room. No longer the year of the would-like-to-be-slender woman, the wish-I-were-flat-chested woman. . . . Cloe bears traces of her old skins. She is dappled and walks giggling through the streets. Here and there, in the play of light and shadow, the variegated patches glow. The soft, ready-to-yield skin, the don't-be-so-oversensitive skin, the I-am-tranquility-personified skin, the sensual-curious skin, the want-to-experience-everything skin. Who can read a dappled skin?

Cloe moves her lips. I am my own woman. People turn and stare. To think that nowadays even young women have started talking to themselves!

Translated from the German by
Johanna Steigleder Moore
and Beth E. Weckmueller

Literally Dreaming

Herstories

What is true to the letter. I dream of an object sailing along the evening sky rapidly approaching. The head of a cow goddess like one I've just seen in an Egyptian exhibition. In the landscape below stands an old farmhouse. It is entirely covered with scale-shaped shingles, all four sides and the roof. Each individual shingle is painted by hand, each in a different shade. Millions of shingles. A voice says: True to the letter. This is true to the letter.

Living the Vita

Especially during the Frankfurt Book Fair, when I meet women I see only during the Frankfurt Book Fair, I am asked if I'm still living in the country, still in that place with the funny zip code, or straight out: Are you still living in that weird place with the four-digit code?

Now, those settlements like Berlin, Munich, and Frankfurt are also designated by four-digit zip codes that all look the same since they all have three zeros. Three times, one after the other, the Egg of creation of the Great Goddess suggests that these particular settlements' inhabitants have an especially good connection to Her. My present zip code, on the contrary, contains three eights. If I make them angular, they become *labyris* standing upright one next to the other representing the creative female trinity, familiar, etched in stone. Looking at the three symbols in my zip code, I think of three *perchtas* or three *hagadisas*, and especially so when I stand at the garden hag and know from my mother's tongue that a hag is a fence and a *hagadisa*, or a *hagazussa*, is a fence rider who can flit back and forth between the worlds.

Around our house ranges the greater celandine, the herb of archaeology that indicates where ruins lie, the herb of eyes and warts. Swallows dribble its juice into the eyes of their young when they are sick, reports Pliny. A little juice smoothed over closed eyelids or a leaf crushed and laid upon the eyes does her good, reports Maria Treben, who late at night, when her eyes are strained from desk work, runs out to the garden to pick celandine leaves. The leaves are matte light green, soft and lobed like those of the oak. The blossom is pastel yellow, and out of the stem oozes thick dark yellow sap almost as orange as nasturtiums or calendula. It's poisonous, leaving stains and causing irritations on the skin. An old saying goes that the herbs one needs begin to grow or are already growing in that place where she lives. But how should the fitting herb grow around her house, in places with four-digit zip codes with three zeros?

I'm also asked: Do you still write?

Constantly, I say. I write about wood and how it would be, finally making the time to gather firewood myself, living this part of my life myself, not having it delivered with coarse words and coarse gestures and coarse truck tracks up in front of our house, from trees belonging to just anybody, which were cut somehow, surely at the right time of year but perhaps at the wrong time of the moon, perhaps as the sap rose in the trunk instead of drawing back into the roots, and surely without being asked if they wanted to leave their lives and become fuel, not merely be felled for timber.

I write about the school, of seeing and smelling, which I have been attending for years. No words can help here even though I have to learn new words in order to distinguish between hardwood and softwood and to experience hardwood splitting more easily than softwood. At least to be able to tell pine from beech from oak in the split logs, to learn how the different woods light, how long they burn, how varied they smell, not just how a fire is made, so that it gets warm allowing me to do something more important than heating the house.

I write about contexts, understanding in the garden how it is, that nothing ever ends but rather keeps on going, that the plants live according to rhythms, affected by radiation I no longer feel and have forgotten, that I used to have so little time after first moving to the country when everything had to be finished and had to be quick in order to be finished quickly, filed away, checked off, bagged, over and done with; that, although I can go quickly into the garden and cut a zucchini whenever I need one, every action has consequences and that the moment I cut off the zucchini will influence the growth of the next zucchinis, either favorably or unfavorably, as well as the zucchinis for next year in the zucchini seeds that I might dry in order to plant next year, and each action in the garden influences the garden for months and years to come. The garden knows no isolated zucchinis needed only for a single dinner.

I'm also asked: What do you do all day? I live the vita, I say. At night watching the teeming worms eating the earth and rotting parts of plants which they channel with worm juice through their long bodies and then pass out again, making earth in which something to eat can grow. Constantly spreading out new food for the worms on the beds, I say, finding in the morning that the wilted nettles are pulled half-underground and disappear in no time when the weather is dry. Imagining a fertile field unpoisoned where under the earth there are so many worms plowing and airing that their weight together is as much as that of the cows that graze above them in the pasture.

Watching the color slowly drawing back out of the red digitalis thimbles under the apple tree, how plants stand there grown high, gradually paling, as one after the other the blooms with the leopard pattern in the chalice fade, before they begin to wilt.

One year steaming the buds of dandelions and preferring them to any artichoke, the next year not doing it, or pickling the buds of cowslips or of nasturtiums to use as capers, the next year not doing it, eating meat one year, the next not.

Opening the front door in the middle of the night because someone is ringing the bell off, seeing calico figures with masks cavorting, giggling, and rattling bells, draped with skins or heavy burlap sacks, and then slowly closing my mouth again because I've recognized a mask and know which friend it belongs to and when she made it, inviting them all in and concocting a soup, listening as they tell that they've been on the road since the afternoon and that they won't get to the last of our houses until four in the morning, wondering who will still open the door for them and who won't, and that Ruprecht on this night of the sixth of December must give back his stolen name to Perchta.*

---

* Perchta/Holle: Frau Holle, Mother Hulda, Mother Holle, Hulle, Holl, Frau Holda, is the spirit goddess of the elderberry tree. She lives in the underworld and comes onto the earth in the time "between the years" (24 December to 6 January). She is the earth mother and has much to do with the weather—when she shakes her featherbed there is snow; when fog rests on a mountain, Frau Holle has lit a fire on the hill. In southern Germany she is called Perchta, the Percht, Bertha. The Percht takes care of the souls seeking new bodies and rides with them through the countryside in the time between the years, the "twelve days of Christmas," on the "raw nights." One honors the ancestress when it is her time, placing food for her outside during this time. (When the Christians took over with Saint Nicholas on 6 December, they made Perchta into Ruprecht, Saint Nicholas's manservant.) Again, she is the spirit of the *elder*-tree, the connection to the ancestresses.

Sitting at the window for hours in the pale moonlight watching the topsoil crumbled on the field reaching plowed-bald to the walls of the house. Sitting for hours on a chair by the window waiting for the vixen that the gamekeeper is hoping to waylay in the woods behind the house.

Watching excitedly how the young fluffed-up swallows learn to fly from the edge of the eaves.

Seeing in each village one of the haggard old women as she stands at the chopping block week after week in the spring and splits wood and stacks it up meter for meter, and in summer, when ours still lies there unsplit, she stands in front of a field planted half with potatoes and half with strawberries, hands on hips.

Learning from women to see and to believe the seeing as earlier the reading and the writing and the counting were believed. Looking for women, words for the word *woman,* and the image of woman in the Long History in which women drafted all the images, which appear in the ruling Short History only as booty.

Helping friends when one is laid up with lumbago on a bed of bracken, cleaning the goat stable, baking a Sacher torte, hearing from the neighbor woman that celery root grows like wickerwork and is good for the nerves, turning the hay, letting the small daughter show me a dead blindworm rolled up in her hand, a young copper-colored one, listening to the voice of the little girl saying relentlessly, why don't you touch it? Reaching out to take the blindworm in the palm of my hand, marveling how soft she is and how smooth, asking: Do you want to bury her? Following her with my eyes as she skips away calling: Or maybe give it to the cat?

Dreaming we retrieve the old statues from the darkness and lay them out on the floor of a room in twilight. Dreaming the earth is moved because we have brought forth the old statues and the snakes can creep out. Dreaming the snakes slither up the statues draping themselves around an arm of stone, of clay, of wood, or they lie alongside them without moving when a woman comes to view the statues. Dreaming word travels quickly that the snakes have returned and have become so attached to the statues that we only notice them when standing directly in front of them. Dreaming that at first we draw our hands back when we bend down to touch a statue and notice that there lies a snake. Dreaming the snakes are as thick as arms, many arms long.

Loving the statues as our companion lovers.

The Older the Better

The older the better. On the lookout for the empty one, the deserted, the abandoned, walking around, surveying, conferring about that which has become worthless, that which the owners have surrendered to the limits of habitability, coming back into those towns, into those gardens with the planted shrubs, and managing in one small corner of the lands that once belonged to us before they burned us.

Natural stones, large, angular, irregular, in the outside walls and the foundations. A wall so thick it measures from your fingertips to your upper arm. Heavy front door—push against it. Smooth worn flagstones in the hallway, as wide as two feet, with cracks. One has loosened itself from its bed of mortar and gives off a clear ringing tone when walked over by four paws or two feet. Low doors, wooden thresholds. Light in the stairwell through panes streaked and spotted from the blowing of the glass. It's drafty. Start at the very beginning. Nothing is tight. No insulation. Nor isolation either. Building material hoarding its stories for decades, for centuries. Three hundred years, they say. Crooked walls, slanted ceilings, corners, niches, cobwebs. Hearing people say it's a real dump, ramshackle, tear it down and build it over, that'd be better.

Where are you from? hearing them ask. Are your folks still alive? How did you happen to land in our town? No men? How many are you guys then? Two, I say. Women. Hmm. The farmwoman thinks it over. That's okay, too, she says finally. There's less fighting.

Don't you have a husband? Aren't you afraid? Who puts your lamps up? Suppose you can do everything yourselves. Womenfriends live here in the area. Oh, I see. Is that a reason to move? No relatives? Womenfriends are relatives.

Constantly being asked: Where are you from? What kind of license plate is that? And in the same tone of voice: Are y'all *terrorists?*

Going through the empty house, smoking out the former inhabitants' ghosts by burning sage, cleaning grafitti and marks off the walls and beams.

Standing in the empty room, conferring with each other, setting the chisel, stopping the time. Stepping into the house's secrets through the walls, under the rotting floorboards, the drooping wiring, in the evenings standing in front of gaping holes, hammered furrows, torn-up floors, farther away from livable conditions than ever before, having arrived at the open building site, in the material, wanting to know how it looks behind the facade *in reality*.

Living for three months around a campfire behind the house without a kitchen, without a table, with a frying pan and two cooking pots coated with that beautiful, beautifully black soot. One pot for stew and one pot for hot water.

Removing a wall.

Watching the companion lover carry away a dividing wall, cautiously, stone by stone, old bricks laid solid as rock face, larger and heavier than those of today. Outside along the wall of the house, stacking the bricks, gift of another earth with other radiation. Winter crumbled some into soft clumps. Pounding the clumps in the mortar, mixing the powder with linseed oil, painting on a whitewashed wall.

Liberating layered walls. Layer by layer peeling, pulling, scraping, the wallpaper off. The uppermost layer of plaster peels off with it; underneath other layers appear, green islands of color, yellow, turquoise, brown, salmon, from decades and decades. Leaving colored patches on one half of a wall, leftover pictures from an old room. Making a new layer for the rest of the wall with the yellow limestone sand of the area.

Mercifully overlooking other walls from which the wallpaper with the bamboo forest hangs loose in strips from year to year. Learning the craft, getting the feel for it hesitantly, watching, imitating, despairing.

Moving infinitely far from finesse.

In the evening, watching my hand in disbelief, as it shakes uncontrollably, while all I'm trying to do is jot down *bread, butter, cheese, wheelbarrow, rip saw, dowels, order sand + cement, work gloves.*

The two of us swinging the pickax for five days above the secret of sewer pipes, straight across the yard one meter deep, eventually standing in the ditch, five meters long, through bedrock, with the big hunks of Jura limestone over which we groaned until we grew to love them, especially when suddenly the pickax gets stuck in a vein of tenacious red clay, and we rest on the pick handles and remember big Patience and big Sarah, and we will remember forever that particular summer of daylong 90-degree heat and the many weeks afterward, in which pipe after pipe was bedded in sand with connections and divertments, where now the sewage runs, under the red tiles of the floor, whose rows and rows my companion lover had spent days on her knees imagining and during the first cold spell got into a sweat about the slope of the floor to the drain in the shower, while I was already sitting at my next building site with the papers and the words.

Getting up from the table up under the roof, bending and stretching my back, descending the steps from the attic down to the hallway through the open front door out into the sun. At every turning of every flight unwinding a coil in the brain, paint, wood, plaster marching by, smelling a fresh layer of paint, mortar, linseed oil. Finding my way back into the body-bound real, into its rules, experiencing tangible rooms, kneading and modeling after intangible sojourns of spirit and mind.

At the hag with a neighbor, discovering after awhile a geographical point in common in a Moravian town from which she stems just like my father. Remembering how we had to tell our parents' hometowns in first grade and how I loved that foreign name Mährisch-Ostrau. The name itself meant mystery to me, not nearby and obvious like Kirchberg and Ersigen and Koppingen and whatever else the neighboring towns were called that the others said. Mährisch-Ostrau, there was a "Mär," a fairy tale in it, things were different there, and it was far away in the east, I could tell that from Ostrau (*Ost* meaning "east"), and it was even farther away beyond a big city that my parents talked about and where they got married, and that was Prague. Remembering how the teacher said when it was my turn, you don't have to say where you're from, there's something wrong with you. But I lived in the same town that my mother had grown up in and went to the same school she had gone to and lived in her language, but my father wasn't yet naturalized in Switzerland; that doesn't just happen from one day to the next, it takes at least ten years. I was outraged. Not because there was something wrong, I was attached to that name, but, rather, because the teacher wouldn't let me say my secret out loud and listen to the tone resound.

Listening to the neighbor tell how it was with the Czechs, with the Germans, first as refugees and then here, in the town. Don't ask, she says, up there on main street, at the building supply place, that's where they assigned me to. And when the trucks came with the cement, who had to shovel? Me. I was the only woman. In those days cement didn't come in bags. Imagine how I looked at the end of the day, you know what cement does to your skin.

Sometimes she calls over the fence: Why do you work so hard? But then she adds: Oh, well, in the old days we used to have to, too. But in the old days that meant: men's work, because there was a war on, or people were fleeing and were poor in any case. But now it's peacetime and affluence. And we're doing men's work.

The apple trees! I hear they bloom more beautifully than roses. I always say, I don't care about the apples if you can only see them bloom like roses!

She stands between bushes and shrubs and snaps dry branches in the twilight. Sometimes she does this to attract one of us, just for a bit of conversation, a sentence or two before she goes to bed. She continues snapping the dry branches until I follow the sound. There she stands in the half-light, still in her flowered housedress, underneath a patterned blouse and under that a white cotton undershirt, ribbed with broad straps. Sometimes she has already let her hair down for the night and stands there with it undone, held only on the sides with bobby pins. It seems to me she fades into the darkness, blending into the dense bushes, as if she is about to depart for the woods above, disappearing silently among the tree trunks. Good night, she says, I'm tired and have to go to bed. She retraces the few remaining steps back to her front door.

Remembering another fence in another year, alone in a little house, many years ago.

Not a Page Left Out

Is anybody home yet?

I'd gone once more to the back of the house in order to close the bedroom door. It could be that I'll show her how I live. In three steps I traverse my realm, niches without doors, and land in the kitchen.

I didn't hear you coming.

The kitchen is too narrow for two. The front door is the kitchen door. When someone enters, she is already in the middle of things, between the kitchen sink and the gas stove. In this small house there is no hallway and no coatrack.

She smooths down her hair. It is dyed blond and teased up high this evening.

Around here we don't lock the front door, she says. We just walk in and call out.

She doesn't want to be seen at my door, I think to myself. Her feet in pointed shoes standing narrowly together on the kitchen floor. When I moved in, there was linoleum that smelled, clammy and sour. I tore it out and freed a red clinkerstone floor. Under her pastel-colored shoes, with the high heels, the floor looks more uneven than usual. It's the joints, of course. Not only does the floor tilt to one side, the stones also need to be grouted again. But I know I won't be living here long. Even if I do stay, I imagine how much nicer it would be in this kitchen which isn't a kitchen to see tufts of grass growing in the weathered joints.

Come in, I say, and gesture with a wave of my hand to the first niche, where there is room for a table and four chairs. I have put out wine and crackers. Outside it is still light. The horses are unbridled and tear at the grass in the paddock in front of the window. Her farm is the only one for miles around with a horse-drawn wagon. She just stands there and looks around. She doesn't pretend that everything is perfectly normal, sitting down and letting her glance wander furtively around the room. Her gaze catches on something, and she remains standing.

So, she says, marveling. Is that simply a branch you picked up in the woods?

I nod and glance up at the curtain rod, too. I think it's pine. I liked the branch because it was so nicely curved. I don't like those straight rods from the store.

And you just wrapped the curtain around it. She continues staring upward, taking the seam of the curtain hanging at the edge of the window in her hand. It is a colorful material, wine red with yellow and turquoise vines.

I am marveling, too. She is wearing a dress pastel-colored like her shoes. Day in, day out, I see her in work clothes and rubber boots, a scarf wrapped around her head, how she crosses the yard with energetic strides, through the stables full of cows and pigs, bending over in the vegetable garden and weeding; hoeing and sowing, plucking and cutting. She is a small-boned, fragile person with remarkably large strong hands.

This is a material they used to use, she says, and turns around. I can recognize it because I wanted to become a dress designer. I didn't want the farm.

Will you have a glass of wine? I ask.

She nods, smoothing over the tablecloth. This is nice, too, she says, and begins to drink in hasty swallows. Did you do the embroidery yourself?

I shake my head and laugh. I don't have the patience for it, I say. I got it in a Chinese store.

Yes, you get around a lot, she says, then you find these kinds of things. I'm an only child and had to start working on the farm at fifteen. My parents were there, but I had to help with everything and learn it all. They didn't want to sell out. I was allowed to go back to school, but only for the farm—homemaking and agriculture. Someone had to keep up the farm.

She empties the glass in large swallows. I refill it.

Are you alone again? she asks.

I nod. My friend left two days ago.

That was embarrassing last week. She looks me straight in the eye. But my sons would never do anything like that. Really, they wouldn't. They're not like that.

She has makeup on this evening, and around her neck is mother-of-pearl, oval-shaped stones, set in silver.

I shrug my shoulders. If I hadn't experienced it myself, I would say, these days that only happens in books, that somebody stands at the window and eavesdrops.

She waves it off. He really couldn't have been eavesdropping. He had one too many, that happens to him a lot.

She bends forward.

And you know, he's not quite right up here—she taps her forehead—and he can't understand that this house has been rented again, after it was empty for a year. They were evicted, he and his mother. Since he had to leave here, it's been all downhill for him, and even his mother can hardly get through to him. This is where he felt at home, he used to come over to our house a lot, too.

He saw a light in the window, I think, and had to come back. One night there is a strange noise in the room as we are sitting and talking, my friend and I, after midnight. We lift our heads. I turn off the light and push the curtain aside. And directly in front of me a man's head is leaning, his profile separated from us by only a pane of glass, leaning so that his ear is turned toward the room and, in the glow of the streetlight, it looks as if he's sleeping or drunk.

I've already torn open the front door, swearing at him shrilly. Where the flashlight was, I couldn't say. Leaps in the dark, splintering and cracking at fences. It must have been at the paddock.

In daylight, the next morning, I go straightaway on official business to see her at the farm, to the front door and not the kitchen door, where I have often gone in and out.

Was that one of your sons last night? I ask without beating around the bush.

She hadn't reckoned on this. She raises her hands placatingly. How could you think such a thing! Not my sons!

You never know, I growl. A fine story. You'd have wondered at it, too.

We both start laughing. Of course, she says. Afterward he came straight to us. I would have come over to your house today to tell you.

Now she sits across from me, the first of the three neighbors living around us.

A long time ago there was a path between the gardens, she says. Then people lived here for awhile that we didn't get along with. So we closed the fence.

What a shame, I say. It always seems so dumb to me, going out around the two houses. A path would be nicer.

She finishes off the second glass.

Tonight I climbed over the fence, she says. Nobody saw me. At home they don't know where I am.

I refill the glass with wine and stand up. In the paddock the farmhand is moving among the horses and barking his harsh commands. It's getting on to night.

Then I'd better close the shutters before I put the light on, I say, heading for the front of the house. Interested, she looks out the window at her own paddock.

Hello, ma'am, barks the farmhand, as always, and puts two fingers to his cap in greeting.

Evening, Wilfried, I call back, and push the shutters closed. I flick the light switch in the kitchen and in the first niche and put a candle on the table.

If I didn't have Wilfried, she says, I wouldn't know what to do. He's coarse, quick to holler, and, yes, he's a bit slow, but he knows us and grew up on the farm and does good work. He's good with the animals, too, even if it doesn't always sound that way.

He just can't drive the tractor, she adds, for that he doesn't have enough up here. She taps her forehead again. That's why we have the horses. And it works out, too.

Can you drive a tractor? I ask.

She nods.

I learned it all. But, you know, nowadays it'd be too much for me. I have the housework, the garden, the parents have gotten old in the meantime and can't do it anymore, and the sons should be able to study, if they want to. None of my children has to take over the farm.

In the evenings I sometimes hear the deep diesel rumbling of an older Mercedes and see a man with heavy steps opening the kitchen door and slamming it behind him.

Does your husband work somewhere else? I ask.

She shakes her head.

He has his own farm, she says, over there, behind the hill. We met, and each of us was supposed to inherit a farm. He didn't want to give up his, and I didn't want to give up mine. It wouldn't have worked out for our parents. She tries to laugh. So we both kept our farms. Maybe that was a good idea anyway, because it didn't work out. So, now each of us has our own home. Sometimes he comes in the evenings, but it isn't working out.

When the sun shines, sometimes I see her parents sitting on the bench on the south side of the house. Every morning, the mother peels the potatoes in the kitchen. Her face is furrowed with pain. My nerves, she says, my nerves. I don't know what else to try. Other than that, I'm healthy.

She stands up, holding onto the edge of the table.

Do you still use the outhouse? she asks abruptly. Her face has become blotchy.

Wait, I say, I'll go with you.

I take her elbow. It's a clear night. She leans on me the few steps to the door with the heart-shaped opening, as if I had always accompanied her like this. I help her in and push the door to. Around us the lights in the houses have all gone out. A warm breeze drifts over from the paddock, smelling of horses and rain. The heavens begin to cloud over with a layer of white.

I never got around to eating properly today, she says, when we're back in the house. There was so much going on with the animals.

I put water on for coffee and get bread and cheese out of the pantry.

You know, the pigs, they have to be castrated. My father always used to do it, it's men's work. But he can't anymore, he's just too old. A couple of years ago he started showing me how to do it. Now I have to do it by myself. And sometimes it's just too much for me.

Can't you give up the pigs?

She shakes her head. I can't do that, financially. Just with the cows, it wouldn't work, I couldn't make it. I always wanted so much to learn a profession. I wrote the best compositions in school, and I was always drawing.

She rubs her eyes awkwardly. I serve the coffee.

I still sew a lot, she continues. I have ideas enough. And you don't have to be able to tell from their appearance where someone comes from, do you?

Her voice wavers, starting to plead.

You can take a shower in the evening and put on different clothes.

Heavy drops begin drumming against the shutters, followed by a real downpour. She jumps up, runs to the kitchen, and peers out.

My hay! she calls out, horrified, My hay!

She opens the door and carefully sticks her head out. A heavy, even droning can be heard.

It's pouring, she says, sitting back down at the table and thoughtfully drinking her coffee. If it's pouring like that, she says, putting her cup down, then I can't go home yet.

She pushes the wineglass toward me.

Do you still sometimes do any writing? I ask.

She nods. Yes, I never stopped. I just use notebooks, and often I don't get around to it. But I've written down all the important things.

I go into the next room and return with a black oilcloth-covered notebook. Her eyes light up.

I know those, those are the kind they used to have.

I nod. It's my mother's, I say. She's been writing her whole life. Sometimes I'm allowed to read parts of it.

Can I see the handwriting? she asks. May I see what a whole page looks like?

I lay the book on the table. With veneration she begins to leaf through it.

My handwriting isn't so nice, she says finally. So regular. And look how much she wrote, she filled up every page!

She passes her hand over her eyes and closes the notebook.

She must be very lonely, too, your mother, she says. If she writes that much. A whole notebook all full, and not a page left out, and every page all filled up.

She was always writing, yes. Early in the morning, when she couldn't sleep anymore. At noon, before she lay down for awhile, she'd write on the notepad she made her shopping lists on and everything that she had to take care of. Quickly holding on to ideas and impressions, stealing small bits of time for little notes. And on evenings when she was home alone, she'd take the notebook, in which she'd put all her notes, and out of the fragments she made full pages in her best handwriting.

She stands up. I'm going to get out my notebook again, too. But now I've got to go, I hope they haven't locked the door yet at home.

We step out together in front of the door. It's pouring.

Do you have an umbrella? she asks.

I shake my head. I don't like umbrellas. But you can't go home like this, you'd be soaked through by the time you got there. Wait here, I say, I'll give you a lift over.

I take the car key from the wall and run to the shed before she can protest. I drive up in front of the kitchen door and let her get in, roll off the property onto the street and drive the curve around my house and up into her yard in front of her kitchen door. We're laughing so hard we can hardly see straight.

If they only knew, she chortles, if they only knew.

She opens the car door. If they could only see me now, how I'm being chauffeured home.

In two steps she is next to the kitchen door, opens it, gives a brief wave, and disappears.

With Head and Hair

The small town with the poor and rich, with the married and divorced and illegitimate, the industrious and the drunkards, the motorcycle rowdies, the inconspicuous, the asocial, the helpful, the generous, the spiteful, the curious, the liberals, those who had the dog that was beaten to death and the other who was poisoned, and the cars broken into and the tormented cats, the small town waits for the men who never enter into the house of the women who live together. The natives and the new residents have too many cuttings and seedlings and shrubs and begin to trade from the spring through the fall. The natives remember that the flowers and herbs that grow at the new residents' house used to grow in their gardens, too, one or another comes by in order to borrow an herb book or to show a plant whose name she doesn't know, and in time they remember, that one's sister, she never got married either and lived her whole life together with another sister and those that lived here before the women, the commune, they used to just open the upstairs window in winter and dump the ashes out into the garden in front of the house where no flowers grew. At the women's, the postwoman says, now there's an ivy wreath hanging on the door. But a man, says the farmwoman, they don't have. They have books and spices, says the postwoman, they can do it all by themselves.

Living without a refrigerator, going down the winding stairs, pushing open the creaking door that hangs crooked on its hinges, standing under the vaulted ceiling, watching a lizard scoot across the floor, searching for a jar with a hand deep in the recesses of the shelf, reaching into something slimy, crying out, jerking back, on the edge of the case of beer, seeing a minute golden-yellow toad sitting there, bending slightly, quiet, selecting the right jar, pulling the door shut, climbing the stairs hunched over without bumping your head, snapping the light off.

Hearing in the night how a falling apple plunks down hard and heavy on the ground, a falling plum a bit more quietly but still with a plop, and finally hearing how a leaf lets go of a branch.

In some years, once a year, listening into the night, and when someone calls out: The wild geese! jumping up, running out the front door, fascinated, hearing from high above the penetrating chatter, thinking of the cranes that I have never seen, whose flight patterns inspired the cuneiform characters.

Hearing in the daytime how the farm machines as broad as tanks take over the entire street, long into the evening, with the squawking radios, how one tractor after another whizzes down main street, how the milk machines drone, how the tank trucks unload the mast every other day with their motors running, how the pigs squeal lethally mornings and evenings, and, in the sky in good weather, the low-flying starfighters shoot along at church spire–height over the stinking dung fields and over our idolatrous love of tomato plants, zucchinis, strawberries, pumpkins, beans, mangold, lettuce, herbs, and the blossoming splendor of flowers.

On a pitch-black moonless night starting awake into a noise that doesn't fit, a rattling of chains and lights that are turning on a tank headed straight for the house directly into my frozen stare and beyond it, passing by a hair between the house and the shed and continuing back into his fall maneuvers from which he'd lost his way. After the paralysis boiling with rage, rushing to the phone, calling up the barracks, hearing the CQ (charge of quarters) saying: What was his number? Without a number there's nothing I can do.

Walking along the yellow pasture where as far as the eye can see no blade of green grows overnight anymore since the herbicide has been used on it from those bottles stored in the cellar whose labels had washed off during the winter flooding, the labels with the skull and crossbones and the directions Do not use in the vicinity of grazing animals. The goat and the kid grazed on, the goat poisoned, in agony for hours, dying. Watching how under the yellow tufts of grass new green grass sprouts while the dairy cows from which we get our milk graze on another pasture for a few weeks. Not going for milk in the evenings for awhile with our can in hand along the narrow path to the cow barn, where the cats are already gathered in the dooryard, waiting for the milk foam.

In the supermarket everything is hygienically packaged and ice cold. The milk is white and inspected. All you have to do is reach out and take it from the shelf. What do I care if it's from cows who spent all day in a barn or if they were brought out to graze or whether clover or yellowed grass was growing in the pasture?

Standing in a corner of the garden in a radius of two steps around me, counting sixty slugs before a thunderstorm. Hearing a woman say, I don't go into the garden without a knife anymore, and her eyes blacken with horror. Once buying a package of slug poison, letting it stand for a year on the cellar steps then throwing it into the trash. Out around the beds, out around the beds, say the neighbor women eagerly, of course not right next to the lettuce.

The poison stays in the earth, I say. The rain washes it out, the rain washes it out, they say eagerly. It keeps seeping deeper into the earth for many years, I say. Well, if you want to be that fussy about it, if you want to be that fussy about it, they say, and move on. Watching how slugs aim directly for tender plants firmly rooted which can't run away and are destined to be eaten alive. For a short time putting up beer traps and learning to loathe beer while fishing slug corpses out of the dishes in the morning, not liking beer anymore because the slugs that I don't like, like the same beer that I do. Onions and garlic at the edge of the beds don't impress them anymore, hardly even ashes, pine needles, sawdust, and then only when it doesn't rain, and it rains a lot and the more it rains, the more everyone is talking about the slugs, on main street, at the supermarket, at the garden fence. When the slugs crawl out of the earth already in the late afternoon that means the weather is going to change or the moon is passing through a water sign of the zodiac which positively influences the sowing of lettuce, which the slugs are so fond of.

It looks comfortable in the kitchen, in the lamplight the companion lover is good to look at as she carves a magic wand, I don't want to change in and out of my gardening shoes, my breath comes out whistling, already it's getting dark outside, can you put some water on to boil? I say, I'll take care of the slugs today.

Sitting awake late into the night in the kitchen in the dark. Through the cast-iron sheet on the wood cookstove runs a crack, it will hold one more winter. Watching the light of the flames dart over the walls and stovepipe, following the thread of memory backward, landing at ground level in the first house in the country, sleeping deeply with window sashes thrown wide open, effortlessly remembering dreams. Sleeping artlessly in a world in which women's fear at night seems to be a law of nature moves things into perspective, *wordlessly* touching the uppermost level of a female order.

In San Francisco I saw a black man sleeping in a car with the windows open, his legs over the steering wheel, one arm hanging out of the window. I stood still and imprinted the picture in my mind. Black man, I said silently, you have been enslaved, and you have been dispossessed. You have been wronged by the white *man*, but I, a free white woman, cannot sleep like that at the edge of the road.

By day in my mind's eye a room surrounded by tall illuminated windows and various pictures in numerous rows on the walls going to my lectern in the middle of the room and like others at their lecterns in the same room silently working on a page on which the calligraphy and the colored pictures alternate as on all the other pages of all the others in the pictorial chronicle of a whole epoch.

Reading about the hole in the ozone layer in the stratosphere above the South Pole as large as the United States of North America. The neighbor woman says, the chickens are now laying poorly in the summer and all through the winter so well, everything is all mixed up. Have you heard? In the reactor there was a screw loose again that they couldn't find. I lay the egg carton with the two-mark pieces in it on the wooden post of the garden fence, weighted down with a piece of Jura limestone, and leave it standing there until she has time to fill it with eggs. If the chickens are laying enough the carton stands there with the top open with one or two extra eggs on top, and when they're laying poorly only one row is filled and a one-mark piece is returned.

One of us walks with the egg carton under the greenhouse effect and the rumors of the ozone hole through the garden in that country with the nuclear missile heads in the ground under the sky with the sun and the low flying starfighters and the swallows who fly high when the weather is good and fly low when the weather is bad.

Gathering up the first apples, cool from the wet grass, haven't bought apples for years. From August to the first snow they stand in baskets in the hall and in the kitchen, exhaling their fragrance, then are carried into the cellar and sometimes they're brought away to be pressed for cider and sometimes they're not and in the first ecstasy, being turned into apple pies for days on end, and all through the long winter they are fetched fresh from the cellar up to the last wrinkly specimens in April when the apple year is over and does not begin again until August.

Living with Holle's bush, going out in May, picking eat and drink, creamy white umbels as big as the palm of the hand, carrying home a basket full of elderberry blossom perfume, spreading the umbels out to dry up under the roof, deep-frying some of them dipped in pancake batter, setting some up to steep with water, lemon slices, and honey and standing it out in the sun in a large stoneware pot, for days, for weeks, for as long as the elderberry blooms, drinking lemonade.

In September the two of us on hot days once again seeking out the bushes with the shiny black berries, the sun warm on our backs, pulling the branches down to us and snipping the heavy umbels off with scissors, bringing them home by the bushel. In the evenings starting to make fires in the stove once again, placing the black enamel juicer on the wood cookstove, which the dialect calls *hexe* (witch), which smells of wood and smoked herbs and stores hot water in the small reservoir, pulling the plug on the electrical water heater for nine months, pausing to reflect at whose place I'll stay during the book fair.

Filling up bottle after bottle with the boiling hot juice for the clammy days, for flu, for lethargy and nervous disorders of all kinds, eating black soup for the first time, in which semolina dumplings swim and apple pieces, drinking the hot juice with a shot of vodka and whipped cream. For days already hearing the starlings in the pear tree picking and gabbing high up in the hundred-year-old branches where no one else can pick anymore.

Hearing from a farm woman that larch needles don't fall on snow. If snow falls and the larch needles haven't fallen off yet, the snow won't stay because larch needles want to lie on the ground, not on snow. Year after year lying in wait to see how long the needles hang on the larches and never finding them on snow.

Watching the hellebore bloom on in the vase, snowdrops, snowflakes, jonquils, narcissus, yellow, white, downy, round, hanging catkins that leave behind pollen outlines on the wood. This siren tone, explains the man on the radio in the language of men on the radio, can be heard in case of a *peacetime emergency*. I can't keep them straight, these emergency tones. If I can hear the churchbells in the neighboring town, the weather is going to change. The man on the radio doesn't know this. He speaks about reactor accidents and the tone for a reactor accident. Purple and white lilac blooms have already poured out their fragrance. Cuckoo flowers, cowslips, buttercups, sorrel, meadow geraniums, marsh lilies, have faded. Peonies slowly drop clusters of petals. The weeks pass by with anemones, daisies, calendula, knotweed, love-in-a-mist, fireweed, chalk plant, devil's bit, willow weed, bluebells, and roses roses roses. Green-blooming alchemilla, meadowsweet, hollyhocks, mountain ash, and with them the first morning mist. Delphiniums make a last appearance, dahlias, spherical, hedgehog-shaped, radiant, pale, deep-dark, glowing red balls, and finally sunflowers.

Standing with the apple in my hand under the faucet as if a film had stopped, unable to decide whether I should eat the apple with the acid rain on it or if I should rinse it off with the recycled water from some dubious processing plant.

Not forgetting the winter when we had absolutely nothing, no house and no food, canned or preserved, but winter is not the right time of year to look for a house, so we found refuge in two friends' pension and had time. There was a central oil heating system, and when it went on the blink because the oil had thickened over night in the cold, the whole house was freezing in no time with no fireplace and no hot water. On the other days it was pleasant in the mornings just turning up the thermostat and mulling over clever thoughts with coffee cup in hand, all four of us were constantly sick, and there was no elderberry juice and no other herbs, only shop counters and cash registers and strange things to buy. It got you depressed.

Witnessing war games.

During the Mardi Gras season reading in the paper: *At three P.M. witch burning in the village square. Followed by the witch's dance.* Calling up the mayor, hearing him say, it's always been done like this, we're only driving winter out. Insisting, why do men have to burn a witch to drive out winter, hearing him say, you shouldn't see it that way, it's only symbolic, our performances are famous, we even had the tv here.

Hearing from a friend that in her area two hundred kilometers to the west they set up funeral pyres in every town, that she had gotten out of her car and gone up close to look at one with a life-size female doll on top, dressed in sneakers and jeans and a blouse like you or me and that's the way they burn it.

Watching my companion lover in sleep with her pictures with which she travels far beyond desire in her yearning body lying in the room.

Knowing where, another place to feel at home, always at the same hour, always at the same spot, and with a name. Basketball. Coming together from all directions. The melancholy and the inventive, the sparkling and the seeking, each and every one a self-willed border wanderer. Sprinting away in an anonymous space, in a gym that smells of everyday school sweat and that reawakens in each woman the old dreads and fears so that she can twist and turn and put them away, breaking away and leaving in the locker room a part of the pressures brought from home, the pile of not-yet-split wood in front of the house, or the space where there's no wood stacked at all, the wants and needs of money, of jobs, of relationships and of existence. Passing the ball between us, not talking, simply playing, simply getting a feel for what the ball wants.

Warm water on all sides from eight shower heads. Closing my eyes, bending my head back, letting the water run over my throat like under a waterfall. Can I use your soap? Anybody bring along shampoo? White tiles from floor to ceiling. Neon lighting. Of all the rooms we meet in, the most sterile and narrow. Soap-smoothed shoulders and backs, thinly coated with a waterskin that pearls off as we turn in turn around one another and do not touch.

In the shower room of a school letting conflicting pictures and feelings storm in on me and in the middle of it, at the nadir of the whirlpool, a sensation of shock at the dignity, the uniqueness with which each of us lives, incorruptible in the way she bends her back, how her hands rinse off the soap, how the water runs off her breasts. At the same time memories of other experiences that are also stored in the cells of my body slit through my feelings, and now the room is a room like countless others, easy to clean, which no one voluntarily enters. Behind the beauty of breasts, bellies, backs, legs, arms, heads, which their own hands caress, I see desecration, next to courage, humiliation. Thousands of horror moments on a threshhold, alone or one of many, eyes and hands in front of eyes that are compelled to terrorize and to mutilate and which hold the compulsion fast on paper and celluloid. In the movies and on tv watching the terror in the shower, where a woman stands behind the translucent plastic curtain, her eyes closed, her throat free. On the other side, the murderer. Compelled as a viewer into being his accomplice, because, contrary to the woman in the shower, I know that the murderer is lying in wait for her. Female bodies manifest political power, store mental, erotic knowledge, the inheritance of the high cultures, indestructible and immortal. Yet the carrier can be vulnerable and ridiculously mortal, as we know only too well. So, we stand under the showers and wash off the sport sweat, each in her turnings and windings under the stream of water and in her own thoughts and feelings. We have willingly entered this room by our own hands laughing and we go out standing tall and laughing again and know there are kin, relatives, images we have created.

Unwinding the thread of memory back to a workroom in Berlin, into an everyday morning, seeing an easel in sunshine, two women standing in front of it, angling their heads to the right and to the left, taking a step back, squinting their eyes, holding up a hand to cover a part of the painting from a distance, and rolling cigarettes all the while. What drives a woman to stand in front of an empty canvas at ten in the morning and to say: I am a painter, now my work day is starting, even if no one knows it, even if no one is waiting for my oeuvre? Into the heart of the fine arts, passing pamphlets, handouts, manifestos, and slogans, through art popes' and papesses' laughter.

Inviting the friends who play basketball, reading to them, how we play basketball and how we stand in the shower, listening to the breathing around me deepen and slow down, feeling how my voice begins to quaver, thinking: *Keep on going!* lowering the piece of paper, being at home among those of my own kind, in life and writing.

Falling asleep in the circle of spread-out, filled-up leaves on the floor. Dreaming that old Hanna stands in the middle of the room, small, with powerful blue eyes and calling as she did in life: Someday you'll think of old Hanna and you'll say she wasn't all that wrong with her teachings, to concentrate yourself on the center of your own energies and not to forget the archetypes. Deep in sleep hearing her trusted voice saying: You've got to piece together the ancient Goddess. But Hanna, I answer surprised, she's been dead so long. No no, she insists, if you descend into the earth, you can put her together again, *with head and hair.*

Working through a researcher's thick book of archetypes, at night, alone in the house, shaking my head, reading about the *negative elemental character of the female** and inducing the period of sleepless nights, scenes full of gorging, jagged-toothed, devouring figures, toads, snakes, vulvae, all mixed up wildly together, and above them all Kali as she dances, teeth bared, on Shiva, with a chain of skulls around her neck.

---

*In Erich Neumann, *The Great Mother.*

I didn't want to know anymore about it then, why do it myself, why bother, I'd rather earn a lot of money and be able to buy what I need, that goes quickly and saves time, and I need the time for the stimulation that I need, and the inspirations only come when the mind is totally free and I as a free person live a totally free life and can drive anytime anywhere I want to where maybe I'll see or hear something that could inspire me, the quiet in the country at night I'd manage with, but the wood business and the preserves business and the garden business, that all just keeps me away from the real arts, I thought.

And That Is the Reason

There's no use complaining that someone is the way she is. Clementine is out of work, Caroline is out of work, but that is not the reason.

In the mornings, the inhospitable cold is the most inhospitable. In the morning the inhospitable cold is like a watchful spirit to wake you or like a leaden paralysis. The life spirits begin to fidget and somersault awake all at the same time, or they curl up and slither along the walls of the soul.

In the morning it is very very cold, it has been cold every morning for weeks, it has been cold every morning for months. No one calls you to work, no alarm clock rings, no appointments press. Clementine arranges her own work schedule, Caroline arranges her own work schedule, that is the reason. It gets light, it gets dark, Clementine arranges her own hours, Caroline arranges her own hours, that is the reason. Outside the windows hangs a curtain of fog or snow, on the branches of the trees there is snow, frost-blooms grow on the panes. The birds cry out, the earth is hard and refusing.

There are numerous reasons to get up.

Clementine, says Clementine's grandmother, get up and heat the house. Feed the birds. Clementine, you've got to heat the whole house from the bottom up. You need bird food, Clementine, in winter you need a lot of bird food, that's the most important. I've seen a lot of nuthatches, bullfinches, yellowhammers, blackbirds, thrushes, sparrows, crows, magpies, jays, and woodpeckers, but there will be more coming.

Clementine's grandmother and Clementine's grandfather live in the attic. Clementine's grandmother has a bird's head. Clementine and Caroline are not surprised, knowing as they do from dreams that things like this occur. Clementine's grandfather has the same face as when he was alive but is quite dead and unredeemed. He always stands in the same corner. Grandmother flits through the house.

There are numerous reasons to get up.

If you don't heat the house, the pipes freeze, the plants die, the animals get sick, but that is not the reason. If you don't heat the house, life does not continue, in no way does it continue, above all, spiritual life does not continue if you don't heat the house. When the kitchen stove crackles and roars, the cycle is once again in motion for the day. When it gets warm in the kitchen, and it gets warm quickly in the kitchen, your desire increases to spend the day in an upright position and not to crawl back into bed.

The snow piles up in front of the windows. In the attic it is snowing, the icy wind from the east sifts the fine flour through the roof tiles. On the shadowy floor under the roof, small powdered islands build up. How good it is to have a roof over your head and walls around your body and deep window seats in niches. If the winter were over in March, the wood might last, but the winter gets longer every year, many weeks longer and very cold, but the winter is endlessly longer and colder in Spitzbergen.

Caroline spends all night reading about the polar night in Spitzbergen, Clementine reads all day about a woman who wants to die and wants to die at home.

Clementine loves the noiselessness with which the snow falls endlessly. How would it be to walk under the snow, warmer than over the snow. The snow is soft and falls noiselessly and covers up all known things and does not disappear for a long time. The snow is a great force and brings the power of the cars to a standstill. The dog comes in with snowflake fur and a powdered sugar snout, she loves the snow, she sits in the middle of it and wolfs snow, gulping it down by the muzzleful. She leaps into the air with joy and dashes off like mad. The cat stretches and stretches and stretches herself, easing out of the kitchen warmth into the white coldness outside in one unbroken move. Caroline shakes herself brr and shivers. Caroline is not a cat and she contemplates a long time before taking a step and that is the reason.

Clementine, says Clementine's grandmother, read for your life and feed the birds. Everything else will take care of itself. Your life will go on for a long time yet and you can be industrious often enough, but for now, pull the covers over your head and read, for my soul's sake, just leave everything and read.

The woman in the book who wants to die at home finally finds it possible to live intensively and to do only what her heart desires. There is nothing else she needs to do anymore other than to know whether her heart desires something or whether her heart does not desire something. She no longer needs to concern herself with everyday things because she knows that she is dying, thus she measures her energy and her time and she no longer misuses her energy nor does she senselessly waste her time.

Oh, Grandmother, says Clementine, I'm depressed, every day there's so much useless talk and I hear everything said every day and the sentences that continually miss one another get caught in my ears and I can't get rid of them anymore and that is the reason.

Clementine, says Clementine's grandmother, if you suffer so from the spoken word, open the book covers and close your ears. If reading is a passion for someone, she should be paid to do it and not have to do anything else.

Oh, Grandmother, I'm so depressed, Clementine says, every day I die and don't know why. I don't have cancer and yet I'm daily dying. Oh, Grandmother, what am I doing?

Keep on living, Clementine, says Clementine's grandmother, keep on living and don't stop reading. When I was as young as you, I did nothing but clean and scrub and polish and nag your mother so that she cleaned and scrubbed and polished too and we were both deathly unhappy and made our lives miserable. When I was very young, Clementine, the only thing I wanted to do was read, and your great-grandmother, when she did our braids up in the morning, made us recite psalms, and if we got them wrong, she pulled our hair out. Your great-grandmother allowed only the Bible, Clementine, the Bible and the cookbook, and all the romance novels that I would have loved to read—Courths-Mahler and Marlitt—she took them away from me. When I married your grandfather, Clementine, I thought, finally I can read as much as I want to, but your grandfather was an educated man and knew how to deal with books; he burned my Courths-Mahler and Marlitt, Clementine, he burned all my novels and my longings and took Gottfried Keller and Conrad Ferdinand Meyer and Jeremias Gotthelf off of his bookshelf and said, Now *we* are going to read something worthwhile, oh, Clementine, all my longing was thrown in the fire and I cried my eyes out. When I was old and he was old and when he died before me, I thought, now I can finally read, I had five years yet, I didn't have to clean anymore or cook, only read, I thought, and then I went blind. Oh, Clementine, everyone had to read to me, your mother had to read to me, and on my deathbed all I wanted to hear were the psalms I hadn't gotten right when I was little, Clementine, read a novel, read to me from a novel and don't stop until you get to the end.

Clementine and Caroline read all the books about survival. More and more books keep coming out in which a woman survives in the wilderness. She has a few potatoes, a few seeds, a piece of land, a hut, a forest with wood, sometimes an animal as companion, she learns to shoot and she learns to hunt. When it isn't winter, she has to prepare for the coming of winter, gather a supply of wood, raise vegetables, harvest and preserve them. When winter comes, she has time to reflect, to dream and to write. She can decide what is important and what is unimportant, because it depends on her whether she continues to live or not and she knows now what is essential and what is inessential and that is the reason.

Caroline, says Clementine, I am dying every day and yet I don't have cancer. I live like someone dying who does only what is important, and partly like in Spitzbergen because the snow is piled up in front of the windows. Caroline, if I look around our town, how they drive those leaden cars through the soft glistening snow that only queens should be allowed to walk on in bare soles without feeling cold and when I see, Caroline, how repellingly pork-ugly most people look because they eat and think so much ugliness and how they all scrub their houses and what they collect in their houses— then I must say, Caroline, we live in this town like in the polar night.

Clementine, says Caroline, I stand at the window and watch the farm women go into their barns, I stand here and am seen only when I take the mail out of the mailbox or when I go get milk or when I put the trashcan out at the curb.

Caroline, says Clementine, there's no use lamenting that someone is the way she is, there must be a deeper meaning. In the meantime, you could learn to understand the language of the birds, Caroline. I spoke with Grandmother today, she thinks it would be the best thing and Grandmother must know, she has a bird's head and has been redeemed.

Oh, Clementine, says Caroline, if I didn't need to prove I'm industrious and have some sort of worth in this horror-filled world, I could open my ears again and hear, but Clementine, I don't like this world and don't know why I'm here and that's why I remain silent and deaf.

Caroline, says Clementine, I stand here rocking my head back and forth. That's not good, Caroline, that's not good, you've got the makings of a politician, you've got what it takes in the wilderness, there are so many reasons to get up, the birds are crying, the dog wants out, someone like you should be mayor, you'd be a mayor with class.

Clementine, says Caroline, it used to be that the water's edge came up to the town, this rise here, where our house stands, was once upon a time a reef, Clementine we live on the reef, I hear the seagulls screaming and smell the salty air, I'd love to eat a piece of seal meat.

Caroline, says Clementine, I need chocolate, I have my period.

Clementine, says Caroline, there isn't any chocolate, there isn't any supermarket, there's no village street, we live on the reef, I hear the seagulls screaming, I smell the salty air, Clementine, I'm the mayor, Clementine, what do you say to that?

As Unquestioning in Daylight as in Dreams

Then I struck out at everything around me and was constantly screaming: I can't stand it anymore, I want a living-silo-one-room-apartment with a garbage disposal, a dry cleaners downstairs in the building, every day a frozen tv-dinner, door shut and decorous table conversation about nothing but literature. In the beginning everything was possible and I always wanted the self-motivated life and a conventional house that turned out to be a place of inspiration, with tenants who are muses and artists.

Then I read over what I'd written down about corpses and about two companion lovers who apportion their own time and work and want to see to it themselves how they earn money and it doesn't matter if they are writers, dancers, artisans, scientists, artists, or life artistes who live for a single idea. "I'm often amazed that these relationships don't run a more lethal course," it says there, and I have to laugh, that's what diaries are for. "It wouldn't surprise me if I suddenly had a corpse in my arms, or if I lay as a corpse in her arms, but corpses don't suddenly happen. Of course a corpse is no solution," I had added, "but as soon as the corpse is there, there's no more companion lover who happens to be depressed when I'm in a good working phase or who's making eyes at someone when I'm not feeling like it or who's gone all the time and is never here or who's always here but can't stand to hear my dubious doubts any longer and suddenly says: Oh, you with your words, for you the only thing that counts anyway are words."

It did take awhile for the obstinacy to let up and the trust to return; before dinner I drove the car to the mechanic's, three houses up the street, up the steep driveway, but he had no time and the windows on the right side were fogged up as I rolled back down the driveway and it was just beginning to dawn on me that the curve to the street was tighter than usual this time, as the left side of the car began to sink. I started sweating and froze at the same time and couldn't do a thing except fall down and imagine that there had never been such a ridiculous situation before, on your own street, three houses down the block, to fall right off the road. Then the moment of panic was over, the right back wheel bumped over something, paint crumbled, and the car stood on all fours on the street.

Then wanting to convince myself that everything would go more smoothly after that scare, I found in my books of the stars a constellation I already knew from my first car accident and when that constellation was dominant I hadn't wanted to go out of the house anymore at all, but now it had passed. I drew myself a bath with wheat bran and balm mint oil in order to cleanse myself of the disbelief and to calm down, but then I quickly ran back up to the attic to take down the herb bundles that would otherwise start getting clammy up there—now that everything was going well again, I had to start right away to get everything in proper order, and knotted an armful of peppermint leaves in a cloth and hung it above the stove to finish drying.

The bath did me a world of good, hundredweights, it seemed to me, dissolved in the water and gurgled down the drain, while I was still standing in front of the mirror blow-drying my hair. But then suddenly I sniffed the air and ran into the kitchen as if stung by a tarantula, following a penetrating herbal smell. The bundle of mint lay on the stoveplate, aflame, and in the blaze I saw all the flammables around me, wooden shelves, wooden floor, wooden sink, the sink too small for the bundle, the bath water just drained out. I reached into the flames and ran with the burning bundle over the woolen rug to the garden door and whooshed it out, where it continued to burn in the grass and ran for the bucket with the flower water.

Then the flu got me after the immolation and forced me to be quiet. I had time to read and to sleep and daydream simplemindedly, and then I had to laugh about these strange spiritual afflictions, until names occurred to me that fit them. I had time to marvel out the window on a day hungover with a strange warmth and to remember how it is to live with firsthand sensations, with true stories, and to feel as unquestioning in daylight as in dreams.

The first three years flew by. What the senses could take in reached me slowly, through many layers, and it took time to combine the call of an animal with a movement and a form and a name; I walked into the winds, following the clouds into the glistening shoals, that was a day's work. Everything was new on the earth and in the skies, a confusion of sounds and calls and colors and shapes, but I could not tell one from the other. After I had been walking for a time over the flat earth, I began to hear in my friend's sentences words that she had been saying all the long short time but which had taken some time to gain meaning and context, oyster catcher, I now made out, lapwing, jay, partridge, yellowhammer, pheasant. I stopped. Which ones are the oyster catchers? I asked.

I jumped around the established garden and hung my heart on every flower, before I even knew anything about it, I threw seeds any old way onto the flower beds and was deliriously happy when something came up, I fought every year with the pile of garbage that was supposed to become compost and capitulated.

And then we didn't know how to go on, we packed the house into boxes and put them into storage. We set out and wanted nothing more than to be on the road, in the south we lived for the first time in the middle of a village, and behind the wall in the small courtyard, the next-door neighbor's head popped up every evening when she put out a small plate with food for us; spinach, green beans, potatoes, and boiled snails that we could not, contrary to all unwritten laws, eat. Saddened, she took them from the plate and replaced them with more potatoes and gravy. She bought white bread once or twice a week, sometimes coffee, sugar, cinnamon, rice. Her husband herded the sheep around the hills, they had a bit of land, three gardens, olive trees, walnuts, almonds, apples, cherries, pomegranates, pears. We bent down with her over the rows of vegetables, picked the freshly opened zucchini blossoms and she made them into a lunch, with a filling of rice, onions, and spices, and set the filled blooms one next to the other in a casserole dish, swimming in home-pressed olive oil. She had sheep's milk she made yogurt out of, and cheese, and of course she had her own wine and her own vinegar.

Reading Greek mythology, speaking the names of moon goddesses out loud for the first time, Selene, Io, Artemis, Hecate, pointing up to the skies and asking the Cretan neighbor, What's that called? She looked up into the white face. *Seleni,* she said. Arriving at the figures behind the words, passing between the letters of *beten* (in German, to pray) and standing in front of the three *Beths*—Ambeth, Barbeth, Wilbeth—which every man of the church still today calls upon without reason or understanding when he says: *So lasset uns beten!* (Let us pray!) in the stolen women's clothing in which he dresses himself with power.

Looking at the stars and into the light that travels in relays of thousands of millennia taking thousands of years to pass through female cultures to reach us.

Dreaming, all ancestresses have become stars like Ursa Major and still shine in the skies with those names that came from Urania or from Artemis, before anyone could show up and steal the voicing of the names, which no one* can understand.

On the way to the temple finding a run-over snake, crouching down next to her in the dust of the street and touching her; she is still all soft with shimmering scales on her stomach like mother-of-pearl, picking her up and carrying her to the temple to an abandoned altar. Waiting the whole day among women for the undisturbed night to fall then attempting with exact images to call innocently upon a power, from the midst of a kaleidoscope of women's lives, halting in the middle of the call, breaking off; suspicious, miles apart from one another standing in the circle, letting go of the hands that are suddenly cold, moving apart horrified, three of us left over numbed on the stone bench in the warm star-clear night, where no breath of air moves, through a rush of wind that sweeps out of an altar room, twirling up and around once and abruptly stopping, startled up out of nothing.

In the museum standing in front of the painted vases and the wonderfully modeled figurines that fit smoothly and still shining into the palms of the hands when the glass cases are opened, and reading from the gestures how the women are conjuring, banning, seducing, raging, casting spells, initiating, birthing, hunting, loving, fighting, ruling, killing, dancing, castrating, oracling, playing ball, making music.

---

*Here the German innovates in using *keine* for *no one,* whose *e* ending identifies it as feminine, in preference to *keiner,* the conventional masculine form. By making *one*'s e bold we have attempted to lend the English a similar feminine gender marker.

Standing in front of the figures with the heads hacked off and the breasts hacked off, viewing a strangely flat torso with two plastered wounds and deciphering the label that the falsifiers of history have put there: *Priest*. Cursing the classical pornographers, no different from today's. Visualizing Hera in front of me, after she had already been tricked by one of the great terrorists, raped and forced into marriage, with golden ropes around her wrists and an anvil around each ankle, hanging in the sky and out of sheer agony screaming into the cowardly silence of the new hierarchy, into which none of the lesser terrorists dare lose her again.

Reading that there were armed priestesses who had weapons in the moonshape of sickles.

We Work Here

The cliffs can look yellow, as honey-colored as it says in the travel guides. In a stone quarry, machines are droning. Climbing would be possible, steeply downward on a foot-wide path through jagged limestone, waves battering against it far below. The day slowly unfolds, scarcely begun, the sun halfway along her path to the zenith, promising southern fullness, blue and hot. She bathes the inner courtyard of the roofless temple in blinding light, suffering nothing next to it, soaking up all colors.

Kim stuck the spade in her backpack along with the day's provisions and used the screwed-off handle as a walking stick along the path. All her life she has waited for this moment. She imagines exactly how it will be. Luckily we're the same size, she always tells Ulli, and can look into each other's eyes at any time.* Ulli, too, has waited all her life for this moment, and, like Kim, she thinks they will make a fantastic discovery together, but the spade makes her uncomfortable. But Kim, she has been arguing for days, have you forgotten that a stone quarry is right alongside and the workers come out at noon to go to the bathroom in the oracle room, and have you forgotten, Kim, how many times a day tourists appear, and while the men read out loud from the guidebooks, the women wobble in their high-heeled shoes on the worn-down flagstones and say *yes oh yes* before they all disappear again with their

---

*In German the women in this story speak in the formal, respectful, slightly distanced mode with one another, using the formal *Sie* form instead of the familiar *Du*.

naked legs in shorts, how can anyone put a spade to the ground and start to dig?

The spade still lies in the pack. Kim sits on a stone step with her eyes closed and leans back. The stone feels smooth and soft like every other day. So, this is the way it is, she thinks, in the center of power, where everyone is capable of reckless enthusiasm. The heavy steps that have broken through the panicked stillness have echoed away.

Ulli, she says out loud, I'm staying. Today for once I don't want to do anything, just hold my ear to the sun, the one that's infected and swollen. I definitely wouldn't want to fight for my life. She hears how Ulli loads the camera. The lid snaps shut. Screams fade away unheard here, says Ulli in a firm voice, I'm staying too. We're fortunate to have found each other without having become I and you nor you or I, but have remained she and she and she and she, in the way we use the formal *you* with each other. She holds the camera up. Kim, I'm starting now. You have to talk to me now, Kim. Listen, speak firmly with me now while I continue, be very firm and cheerful.

Ulli sets the focus, points the camera at the block-shaped corner seat on the other side, to the left of the middle portal. The eye of the camera wanders over large feet, two pairs of large feet in coarse boots. Ulli presses the shutter release. The eye of the camera closes, spits out the picture, wanders on. Gun belts, two, under fat bellies, too tight, sweaty shirts, the buttons straining. They have laid the guns down between them, in the sun the metal casings flash. The eye of the camera closes and spits out the picture. Ulli walks slowly toward the men, the camera in her hand, looks at unshaven, feisty faces. She gives the hint of a nod. We work here. I'm taking photographs. She points to the portal, the corner seats to the left and right of it, the semicircle of the inner courtyard, she remains standing.

The men blink, grin uncertainly. Oh we have to work here too, goads the one. Then slowly they stand up, sauntering off to the side. The guns lie on the stone seats. You do that wonderfully, Ulli, Kim calls out, stick with it. Ulli points to the guns. They disturb the picture, she says. One of the men saunters over, picks them up with an irritating slowness, saunters back to the other. Ulli peers through the camera eye at the well-known setting of the silent portal with the massive top plate that lies there as if it were sleeping in the sun, reaching out to new weatherings. Ulli takes a step back, the blocks to the left and right of the portal with the seats that feel like smoothly polished ceramic tiles butting into the picture. The two outer sides are densely covered with small hollowed-out bowls. The men stand behind her, she feels their breath as they crack jokes. She sees the bowls sharply focused, they could be honeycombs, also covering the slabstones standing vertically between the portals.

Kim, calls Ulli, the bowls are as innumerable as the stars in the sky. She moves step by step backward, pushing the men toward the exit. We have to work here too, the one razzes again, standing still. Ulli points to the left portal. Here, too, the front edges of the supporting slabs and the top plate are studded with bowls. Get out of the picture, orders Ulli, I want a shot of this portal. Ulli, you know, calls Kim, there aren't any guards here. This is the only temple on the whole island without guides, without entrance fees. Kim gets up and walks back and forth declaiming loudly in the courtyard. Here there is no guide who says during the tour: Here is where the women sat, over there the men. The women sat lower than the men. They had to obey the men. Here they waited until the priest opened the temple.

Kim, calls Ulli, the eyes up there in the portal see everything. The second entrance behind the left portal is like a window opening cut out of a whole slab of stone. Out of the middle of the lintel two deep bowls peer down like eyes on those who stand before it.

The men saunter back to one of the corner seats, conferring quietly with each other. Ulli turns to Kim and inspects the opposite wall of the courtyard, jointlessly rowed slabs standing vertically, the small rectangular opening behind which lies the oracle room. In our temple here, Kim, she says, no guide walks up to you and says conspiratorially: It was the fertility cult, you know? Here no guide points to the tall slim column and says: This is the phallus! and in the same breath gesturing theatrically: Me! And you're the woman, get it? Kim, don't you double up with laughter, think how serious the situation is. The men get up again, uneasy. We have to work here every day, says one. The other puffs out his chest: We are the temple guards. Ulli grips the camera with both hands. Kim, she says, I didn't get to be thirty years old to back off in front of liars, what do you think?

Kim sits back down on the stone step. Here is my home, she declares. Besides, I have to let my ear heal.

Ulli turns to the men, points to the guns. What do you shoot? she asks. She envisions in front of her the creek that flows behind the rented bungalow, with the decoys in the bushes. Men march with shouldered guns through the cattails. On the weekends shots ring out from morning until night all over the small island. Oh, just birds, the men say, as if with one mouth. Every man here has a gun, and every man shoots birds. Kim has gotten up and is standing next to Ulli. What kind of birds? she asks. Are there big birds here?

The men grin. If we get big ones, then we shoot big ones, one says. We bring them home and our wives cook them. They guffaw. Every man here does it.

And if they're little birds? Kim interjects heatedly.

Oh, the little ones, we lock them up in cages.

But you can't lock them up in cages after you've shot them down, Kim parries stubbornly.

Oh no, when we shoot the little birds, we throw them to the dogs.

Ulli raises the camera again and motions with her free hand to the exit: We really must be able to work in peace. It is an order. Hesitantly, the men shoulder the guns and move on.

Ulli pours tea. So that's it, she mumbles, my hands are shaking. It's not surprising, Kim, she continues, lost in thought, that they used to throw themselves from the cliffs, if it's true that it happened, one after the other, fifty of them in less than a minute. And the pursuers breathless, swearing from the heights down toward the depths where the waves closed over the saved bodies.

They scramble over the altars up onto the outside walls, each walking around them once in opposite directions. The apses lie there abandoned, the tall stone blocks keep their secrets calmly to themselves. In the oracle room there's another fresh pile of shit, says Ulli, as they stand next to each other again. Down along the path they've already set up the live decoy cages, says Kim. Soon they'll put up the nets for the birds migrating from Africa. I'm leaving before then.

Ulli lies on her stomach on the stones, looks down over the dark blue unmoving sea. Kim, she says dreamily, they would have been fantastic pictures. I've never seen it so exactly before. Kim's eyes widen. But Ulli, I heard you open and shut the camera. Ulli rolls over on her back, squinting. I didn't put the film in, it had to go so quickly. And those two, she motions vaguely in the air, those two I wouldn't have wanted in my camera. Today the camera had to spit out, not take in.

Arriving in Her Story

Loving the cards, spending hours doing readings and fevering over the pictures, reading a herstory book containing all the true secrets, with the sequence of the beginning, with the numbers of the beginning, with all the women, the Magician and the One, the High Priestess and the Two, the Empress and the Three, and here begins the weakness of the German language which degrades this card to HERRIN and HERRSCHERIN,* the Lady of the Ladies, La Dame Habonde, He Era, the Earth, Woman of Abundance, Hera. Understanding the gesture of the Priestess, who should turn around in the picture on the fifth card with an ear of wheat in her raised hand and lead back through the experienced mysteries to realities of matter, arriving before the secret of the room behind her, without a picture.

Reading in the small print that Hera always fought and never forgot, in the very end, in her old age, she found her place with Artemis, she would sit there in the evenings behind the temple next to the statues of girls with bird legs, while from a distance the noise works its way through to her, the noise Hercules makes to draw attention to his heroic deeds. She dreams of the statues of girls with bird legs, and, when a starfighter roars over the temple, she furrows her forehead for a moment in her dream.

---

*Herrin is the feminine form of Herr; Herrscherin is the feminine form of Herrscher. Herrschen means "to rule" or "to rule over someone." (Compare the noun and verb forms of the English lord.)

Arriving in her story and in the design of her own story, stepping out of the calendar, arriving at the summer solstice across from the winter solstice, arriving at the second of February across from the second of August, arriving at the thirtieth of April across from the thirty-first of October.

Through the open window a soft morning streamed into the room carrying a small feeling of luck, I saw the black squirrel for the first time again, how it swung through the crooked plum tree and suddenly sst! swinging itself from one branch to a branch of the pear tree and back and forth through the soft blue air framed by the window square.

What else is there to do but speak a wordless tongue with individual creatures, as if for the last time?* In bursts life returns as if an incredible undertow had caught it fast on the still visible horizon of the last year. Unbelieving, wandering through the woods, through ankle-deep, kindling-dry leaves, and murmuring foolishly: This is how Easter was as a girl. It was warm, with just this warmth, the cuckoo called from just as far away in the woods. The white anemone blossoms covered the brown leaves, ruglike, the periwinkles bloomed just as blue. Lilies-of-the-valley, bear leek? A field of furled green leaves, unbroken. Conventional feelings return with fervor, resurrecting a world before the senses, one they're accustomed to perceiving, as a conventional stone wall that warms itself in the conventional sun as the conventional grass that greens and grows in the conventional manner. But in the spring a year ago, what did we eat then? Conventional feelings latch on to every green blade of grass, every green leaf. Addicted, savoring every perception, breaking out in rapture over every cowslip in the grass, over every blue crowfoot. As if it might all be over at any moment. Programming every perception into memory. The reality behind the moment will be unconventional, perhaps as in dreams and perhaps transparent, as thoughts can be. Perhaps differently transparent, not merely extinguished, as reported in Hiroshima after that one unconventional moment, when only the outline of a body was reflected briefly off a wall.

The round smooth, the ribbed, the hairy, the angular, stems of the plants lie temptingly in my hand and promise me happiness, if I only want to be happy that they are growing again. The mirror-

---

*The Chernobyl disaster took place one year before this writing.

same happiness in the tangible world, on the other side of the transparent thoughts that create a different kind of happiness with their transparency.

On the other hand, to materialize the thinking black on white, to hold on to it visibly, seems to me cumbersome and dated like any kind of reality that we hold on to or have when we say *we have*. *We have* a reactor here, too, thirty kilometers close as the crow flies and slightly farther away following conventional roads that are so earnestly paved and who try so movingly to do their thing properly. They lead over a number of gently rolling hills graduating the apparition of white cloud which always gathers above the reactor.

Will you come along to gather yarrow on the Ipf and from the Steinernen Jungfrauen, the St. John's wort is blooming, next to the Jungfrauen there's wormwood down on the one pasture and thyme up along the whole slope, we could take along a bit of mole's earth to vaccinate the garden.

Drummers walk the earth as if they were walking on a drum, so they go with the drums in their arms to the Hungerbrunnental and stand in a circle around the spring. We stood there then and drummed, they reported, for two hours we stood there and drummed, the starfighters shot over us, men and women tourists gaped at us, little girls and boys ran yelling around us, we stood there and drummed as if to arrive at this place, to take the same path again and to arrive, to arrive in order to reclaim this place and stay.

From the top of a hill, looking into a valley with a stream winding through it, yellow clumps squatting on its banks: cowslips. For five kilometers not a single house. Fishponds where sometimes a heron appears.

After eleven years arriving in front of that heap collecting for the compost, wanting to invest time in it so it can make good earth, walking over to the farm across the way, asking for horse manure, perhaps in the twelfth year I will dare to make earth as a delicacy, out of pure nettles, the crème de la crème for strawberries and roses.

In the summer calling up the drummer, thinking of her room where the silent drums stand, tall and short ones, goathides stretched over them, the fur-covered edges draped over the rim, in summer writing about the caves, while I pick rosebuds and spread them out to dry, black mallows, mullein and lemon mint, golden mint, peppermint, sage, binding them into bundles together and hanging them up under the roof, where they twirl in the draft, Do you want to drum I ask, while I write, like the way you drum when someone dances or when someone is sick? I pack my things, take my sleeping bag, and set out with the car over back roads, past the house with the wood facade where they're putting in the new bay windows, through the town with the old garden walls with nasturtiums creeping over, through the maze of bypass roads, traffic jams between the low smalltown houses, and finally up the narrow street that seems to lead straight to heaven, up to her house. When she laughs, the she-wind herself carries the high tones over the crest of the hill.

In one of the caves a woman was raped, reports a woman weeks later who is visiting and heard about it from a woman who lives in the small town in whose paper a three-line notice stood.

From the highway a sign points into a side valley to a hill with a crown of pale stone blocks on the summit and sheep who sometimes graze on the one side of the hill and, on the other side, the deep crater of a stone quarry where dredgers drive in and out every day. The cave entrances are scarcely visible from the outside, and sometimes some-one passes by without seeing them, even though she's looking for them.

That reminds me, one says, I saw some porno magazines the first time I was there, I'd completely forgotten. They were lying hidden in a niche at the side, now I remember.

The path leads slowly through cropped-off spongy pasture lands. The hoofprints of the sheep crowd over one another in the softened earth. It smells of thyme, the harebells are blooming be-tween limestone chips and juniper bushes. Out of the earth towers rugged bone, visible from far away, smooth gray stones. I like this path the best, she says, I haven't been up here for half a year. This is my first time here.

We can feel the gentleness of the valley, the age of the stones, dated around fifty thousand. At the entrance to the larger cave there is a sign explaining that the skulls that were found here, mostly children's, all stood on the ground facing west, together with four thousand Mediterranean snails and two hundred stag teeth. The floor of the cave is wet and slippery, sheep must have been here. Step by step, we go into the cave, still in the light. High up in the indiscernible darkness, the bats begin to squeak. We go all the way under the dripping from the ceiling through to the back and stand still. I barely recognize her, she whispers, it's as if she's been plun-dered. She cradles her smallest drum, leans against a wall, caresses the drumskin as if she were caressing the cave. I smooth along the walls, over cracks and folds in the stone, push myself slowly into a side tunnel until I reach a niche from which I can no longer see the main chamber nor the exit. Neglected, I think, unloved. The dread creeps up on me, the angst I was afraid of, a wretched sadness, no sound from the drummer gets through to me. It seems that I no longer know how long I have been in the cave nor if anyone else is here but me.

Slowly we grope our way back out, silently retrace the path to the car, and drive the hour we needed to get there back again through the countryside, through the falling darkness to her house, and there in the music room she stands at the drums and bundles her impressions from the cave, while she drums and I write, how we are always going back to the cave, when morning begins and when evening begins, until the cave has recuperated and any woman can stay there as safely as in her own garden. I hear us sometimes giggling, while I write, in a scratchy hoarse way, as if we were feeling toward that point behind the lamenting and the exorcising. I write how a number of us enter and distribute ourselves throughout the cave, how we lift and lower our feet and begin to stamp, how we stamp the earth of the cave until every foot's breadth is freshly covered, while we hiss, rattle, boo, ohoo, shoosh, lall, growl, coax, click our tongues, whistle, whiff, puff. Each time one of us stays inside as long as she wants, protected by the others who distribute themselves outside and wait. She can go all the way to the back, she can stay in the middle of the cave with her back to the entrance, and she senses how the spirit of the cave with wings spread hangs over her and makes her understand: *I challenge you with fear,* while she breathes through the sightless darkness into the cave walls and into the cave ceiling and realizes how the cave begins to breathe back into her, and to accept her breath when she exhales, always deeper into the fear and there in the protection of the others, she can follow the spoor of the secret that waits, sparkling and mocking, behind the fear.

On the Ipf, the old mountain plateau with the dance floor on top, walking along the edge when the sun is at her highest, at the northern point singing the highest vowel that later transforms itself into a vertical and later still into the letter *I,* and when the sun stands at her lowest point and the bow bends near to the earth, at the southern point singing the deepest vowel, which later moves back up with the opening of the bow to the isolated *U,* walking and singing back and forth from *I* to *U* and from *U* to *I* through all the arguments of the learned, which vowel belongs to which point on the calendar of the year, stepping out of the calendar and calling until the *I-U* becomes an *I-O* and I stand at the points of the sun in the north or in the south and repeat the ancient call Io! Io! Io!—the old name of the moon in Argo, after which the Ionian Sea was named.

It was raining then again after it had rained all of May and half of June, had rained enough in July too, and in August it had continued, it would get nice then for half a day and then rain again in the night until the next noon, then the moon was full opposite the sun in the sign of the Lioness, I turned around and saw a crisis behind me. I sat down with my companion lover in the red currants, we picked the berries, a neighbor came and told stories, I wanted to make jam, to smell the aroma that won't return until the next canning, watching the pink of the foam that cannot be bought bubbling up, skimming off the foam with a foam ladle, letting it flow into a shallow dish, tasting the abundance. I wanted the book to be finished in order to read it, but now I just wanted to sit there for an hour and pick berries and in the hour of the sun to believe the belief that was returning, to believe in something in common sometimes, two companions lovers in the country and others around them, what is that.

For a friend who is seriously ill, preparing a fire. The fireplace is soggy and abandoned, overgrown with clumps of grass, I clear it out, piling on paper, small sticks, and dry branches, strewing a circle of yellow sand out around the stones, farther out a circle of salt. My companion lover whirrs with the whirrwood, I stamp the ground counterclockwise and clack two stones together, so that the life spirits can hear me when I call out the name of the sick one. How could I take part in a Fleuropritual even if I happen to have enough money but don't know what kind of flowers are to be delivered, which I have not seen but, chances are, come from Africa or from South America, with tears and poisonings and skin rashes still clinging to them from the women workers who have to breathe in clouds of insecticides before the tons of dead flowers can be loaded deep-chilled onto planes that fly many times a day solely so that we can order any kind of dead flowers fresh at any time and bring the floral magic into our establishments.

How can I feel life spirits without being able to make a fire inside or outside, without seeing and hearing the flames, without smelling the wood, without burning the herbs, without seeing the smoke rise or knowing how it blows from the stovepipe into the flue and into the chimney and through the whole house and out the chimney pot into the air? How can I live without hearing the wind rushing and howling in the chimney, without being able to tell the stove anything, without the blackened wood ashes to look at the next morning and the white ash hill over the red burned-out coals? The ashen countenance of the fire that speaks wordlessly reminds me of the white countenance of the stone figures that timelessly represent the circle, and the movement of the circle, before a vertical line appears there and divides the circle into two halves, two halves of the year, two halves of the real, like daydreaming and nightdreaming, long before it is fitting to say nose to it or face, except perhaps the face of the year's cyclical motion, the face of the laws, the face of the contexts, faceless, wordless, without form.

In the beginning of August, the windowpanes began to fog up at night, and my mother looked fragile, smaller and thinner than ever, and the hair was light again from the white strands, the order forms from the blind library lay around now, and I told her how long it had taken me to realize her secret, up until that evening when I was visiting with my friend and we showed her our diaries with the drawings and watercolors, and how pretty we found the combination of writing and pictures, and how she didn't react much at all to it, because she couldn't stand to keep her secret anymore and finally the situation was just right to air it. She simply said: I have something like that, too, while she was already on her way to get it, there were numerous notebooks that she had bound together into one, and it was all fifty years ago or older, at first fifty years ago in Paris, when she wrote everything down, what she experienced and thought and painted, how her room looked and the view from the room, and later, much later, she began to write down the twenty years before that, and no one in her family knew that she always had a secret and that there was a drawer for the secret and a key that she kept in a secret place and that I was filled with an unbridled pride, and she nodded contentedly.

It was not finished then, but it had to be finished, because an ending was planned, the end is publication. When the writing is over, a book can appear, but only if the writing stops at a point in time and this must be agreed upon, for the ending is arbitrary, but it could never be any other way. At the end everything crowds together, and suddenly it must all go very quickly, and yet any day the whole thing could take a new turn.

In the mornings and evenings making a fire behind the house, wrapped in a woolen blanket on the days when it isn't raining, keeping a pot of soup warm, sitting on a tree stump beside the coals. Gathering wood on every walk through the woods. Collecting orange crates from every supermarket.

From the second to the fifteenth of August arriving in the basic form* of the verb and using it to write myself out of the labyrinth.

Arriving at the edge of the woods at the side of the four-pawed on a leash, feeling how she tugs and noses out and with every thread of her wiry body is animated only by the woods and by those who live there that she wants to hunt and sensing myself loud, blind, and without feeling.

Going up to the woods at the side of the aesthete on a leash, leaving the feeling in the houses behind me, the feeling with which I decide in the garden where the roses and lilies are to stand, where the annual, light ephemeral summer flowers are to go, where the herbs that are supposed to become large bushes will stand, how between the colorful aromatic blooms the vegetable beds are to go, and which plant wants to stand next to which other plant and which not, and which plant wants the leaves as fertilizer from which other plant, while I passionately forget the time.

Leaving the styled rooms behind me, the aesthetic table, the aesthetic transparent beautifully formed glass bottles and flat bowls and flacons with the essences and fragrant oils and waters and herbs, the set-up tinctures and the blooms and leaves and root pieces that gradually dissolve in alcohol, mixing their colors and smells.

At the side of the four-pawed on a leash, following the desire to go in on no trail, between the tree trunks over the soft ground and the green clearings ever deeper, simply, out of love.

Not gathering bracken for the garden beds in winter or leaves for the strawberries or periwinkles for the slope or pine cones for kindling or wood for heating.

Following the aesthetic, which orginally meant "feeling," with which female dogs and female hunters followed a scent.

Walking in among the trees as in among the letters. In the layers of leaves spread out, falling asleep on the ground.

Loving the trees like the letters.**

Translated from the German by
Johanna Albert and Tobe Levin

---

*Translators' and author's note: if German had a progressive verb form, this book would have been written in that form. Since English does have it, we three have chosen to use it in the English translation.
**The German word for *letter* is *Buchstabe*, literally meaning "beech sticks."

Euphoria
and
Cacophony

Euphoria

This essay is based on a talk I gave at the fifteenth anniversary celebration of Lillemor's Women's Bookstore in Munich/Schwabing. My deep affection for this particular place stems from many things. The assortment is remarkable. I know I can find there an illustrated text by Georgia O'Keefe, poems by Eva Strittmatter, and even so rare a volume as a monogram of Ma Rainey, mother of the blues; I can range from Gertrude Stein's Lifting Belly—"Of course we have it in stock!"—to Zora Neale Hurston to Anna Livia's latest. The bookstore is an enchanted cave, witness to the caring hand of its book-loving owners in all its appointments, and more: it offers a stage for communication. Lillemor's is a woman's place, where I can feel equally at home as an author and a lesbian, one of those rare sites that conveys the feeling of what it would be like to be able to come home.

I can remember when we didn't have any of this, and times were rough. In 1967, when I completed high school, Monique Wittig was thirty-two and had already published her first book, *Opoponax*, in 1964; it won the Prix Medicis the same year that Christa Reinig was honored with the Bremen Prize for Literature. Yet even today the two can't read each other because Christa Reinig's books have not yet been translated.* And back then no one had ever told us these authors existed. We hadn't heard of Virginia Woolf or Marieluise Fleißer, either. And I can't remember ever having heard of a black

---

*Since I gave this talk, *Idleness Is the Root of All Love (Mussigang ist aller Liebe Anfang)* has appeared in an English edition (Calyx Books, 1991).

woman author during my school days. Lessons were traditional, and, after 1968, the Left called for the death of bourgeois literature. The only thing that counted took place in the streets, in the overflowing pubs, in the movies, and in protest songs. Only in 1972 did I begin to read again.

And together with other women I discovered how starved we were, how we were living in times of famine. We wanted to appear as subjects, not as objects of description. We wanted to know what Virginia Woolf had already speculated in 1928, the meaning for modern literature of the sentence "Chloe loved Olivia." Or that Doris Lessing had written about a protagonist wondering whether a menstruating woman might appear in a novel. And where were the women pirates, explorers, guerrillas, founders of nations? One of the most important words we taught ourselves in the early 1970s, at least in my view, was *expertin*, the idea of the woman expert. We realized one day that we were assuming ourselves experts, experts on our bodies, our sexuality and the interpretation of our sexuality, our spirit our psyche our dreams and the interpretation of our dreams; we are experts in our creativity and our production. Thus, we began to speak to one another. We wanted to define anew a female's experience of the world, to put into our own words what the world meant to us. I can remember a text that reached us from the U.S. women's movement and began with the following words: "Our bodies are being used to sell goods that earn men millions." Such a sentence had appeared nowhere in our scripts. One woman opened another's eyes and ears. Each let the other know which perceptions were normal for her. Each began to seize her own existence, because she had begun to hear, read, and pronounce sentences encoding her reality.

Suddenly, we had books. Those who said they knew what literature was and hadn't stopped reading tipped off the others. *The Bell Jar, To the Lighthouse, A Room of One's Own.* In the movies of the counterculture we stared at the screen until after midnight. Appearing there was a powerful head with hair cut short. Even when she was alive she looked like a statue, and she was a writer. And not only did she write but also lived for decades with one and the same female lover. The film was called *if this you see remember me.* For days afterward I ransacked bookstores. The era of women's bookstores had not yet opened. I stumbled across a copy of *Three Lives.* For weeks we lived in those three lives, and especially Melanctha's, just as we lived the life of Christa Wolf's Christa T. for weeks. And no sooner had we recovered from *The Dialectic of Sex* than we discovered *The Female Eunuch, The Myth of Vaginal Orgasm,* and then *Rubyfruit Jungle, Riverfinger Women,* and *Flying.* The slogans also flew from country to country, continent to continent. "A woman without a man is like a fish without a bicycle," we read in France; and with the line "I want a women's revolution like a lover," Robin Morgan began her poem "Monster." The sentence unfurled like a banner from the tongue: "I want a women's revolution like a lover." In the beginning we were all sisters. And the beginning ended quickly. Then it became: "Sisterhood is powerful. It can kill you."

But I'm anticipating myself.

Let's reside awhile in that moment when we said Sisterhood Is Powerful and everything seemed possible. The fever of launching something new was contagious. If we didn't want to remain invisible and inaudible, we would have to make ourselves appear, our voices loud. Everything was happening for the first time, as we shaped reality. Lillemor's Women's Bookstore invited me to give a reading at their opening. It was the first reading of my life from my first book; *Shedding* had appeared in October 1975. As an author, I am therefore as old as Lillemor's, a fact that binds me with special force to the place and the women who run it. We were unutterably excited! And the founding mothers even paid for my flight from Berlin to Munich so that I could read. That in itself excites you when your monthly income is just under $200, not unusual then, and when a shop has just financed itself entirely from loans. But we thus changed reality by simply doing what we did. And suddenly we had everything, our own publisher, our own author, our own book, and our own bookstore. And at that moment we were enthusiastic and proud, for an hour, for the duration of the zero hour. It is the feeling you get when you're between two states. Dreams and wishes have become reality but have not yet been tested in time. Whether you'll make it through crises and feuds, splits, factions, and competition remains to be seen.

What binds me equally strongly, if not even more strongly, to this particular bookstore and those associated with it is the fact that, over the last fifteen years, our affection for one another has not only endured but increased. We all know how many struggles and wars broke out within the women's movement following the first euphoric years, how many projects lived only short lives, how many bitter feuds we have witnessed and still suffer within projects. Lillemor's, too, had its share of troubles and, like all the others, overcame the worst by means of group psychotherapy, not merely to overcome but rather more, to remain as much alive as a cultural space for women as at the moment of its birth. They wanted to continue encouraging and inciting and, in the midst of all self-inflicted turbulence, to continue leading a turbulent life. They have succeeded. From the spark of one generating moment a fifteen-year history has flowed, and it marks our collective history, a history characterized by such euphoria as existed at the birth of the new women's movement, including everything belonging to such an era: too many appointments, everything organized by ourselves alone, the ability to answer all questions, and in the evening, whenever possible, to stand behind a book table at someone else's event. Everything organized, printed, announced and, seen through to completion, whether reading or exhibition, demonstrates an unmistakeable polished Lillemor's style. For their untiring efforts (despite fatigue) and their irresistible charm I wish to give thanks. The fact that we still have with us this sort of collective work is testimony to our own reality and gives hope for the future. And it is every bit as necessary now as fifteen years ago.

I also think that the particular attraction of a woman's bookstore lies in the fact that here the multiplicity of feminist lesbian worlds comes together in one space. Books whose authors may not have known about one another, may have fought or even today remain in ignorance of one another's work, themes that may be mutually exclusive, stand harmoniously back to back and all together fill a room. The booksellers may, of course, decide to spotlight one area or another in an attempt to gently influence the taste of refractory clients. If all too many pounce on the science fiction and don't seem to care for "what's important," the politics section is pushed a little closer to the front and fantasy toward the back. And as for normal, everyday life, Margurerite Duras has a lot to say, if you care to read it. Maybe, at night, certain female spirits escape from your pages in search of adventure. And not only through heaven and hell in the Himalayas. Marlen Haushofer's Meta will finally be joining Julie of the Wolves on a hunting trip, maybe meeting along the way Quila on her way to the thirteenth moon and Mick who knows that The Heart Is a Lonely Hunter. And—if my eyes don't deceive me—there's Rosa Luxemburg in a tête-à-tête with Marion Zimmer Bradley of the shining eyes and utopian systems, while Elisabeth the First, Semiramis, and Amaterasu redirect affairs of state.

Thus, it's no wonder that the bookshop clerk who first arrives in the morning to open the window, brew the coffee, and without too much enthusiasm reach for the vacuum should grow a little weak in the knees. It's not that she's had too little sleep, too much or too little champagne and coffee, no, it's the effects of those nightly indescribably female conferencings she feels.

Cacophony

Then what will you do?

As a veteran of the new women's movement, I'm regarded as a symbol of the outbreak because I wrote *Shedding* and because *Shedding* was the first literary text to come out of the contemporary movement in Germany. With it we mark the history of a book that was also an event. The market didn't make it, protect it, or launch it. Readers' hunger for such a text pushed the printings skyward, which in turn insured the survival of the publisher, Frauenoffensive. The history of *Shedding* is an inverted one.

For me it is above all the history of the author I have since become. In 1977 I wrote in the afterword to the second edition of *Shedding:* "[This] is not the first installment in a literary career. Writing a book seemed at that time to be the most effective form of feminist activism. It doesn't mean that a second will necessarily follow."

After the shedding comes the identity crisis. As the number of *Shedding*s continually climbs, together with the euphoric and wrathful reactions to the ever increasing printings, an identity crisis ensues. Inner paralysis takes over, although at the time I'm not yet aware that later I will so name this epoch. Time seems to have fallen into a vacuum, as nonverbalizable and indescribeable as in the era before *Shedding*. What cannot be said hurts now in another way because in the meantime I've learned that I *can* write pieces of it. What I have written has been heatedly discussed. This sensational success triggered envy, competition, avarice, intrigues, corruption, betrayal, and blockades. Fear snatched my tongue. This new speechlessness causes chronic pain, anesthetizing all my creative impulses. A part of my consciousness is only too readily occupied by wishing the pain would cease. The pain goes on. It kindly ossifies. My newly born knowledge freezes within me, my experience of whole nights spent feverishly writing, of haunted, inexorable writing, of the feeling of wanting to and being able to write. Self-doubt that had periodically tormented me and the momentary fear of publication couldn't stop the writing. Ossification now seems to be erasing me. I kick and punch but can't break out. Years of despair can't soften it. I'm too impatient and inexperienced a writer to understand that this paralysis is needed to protect my writing from destruction from without and thoughtless, hasty wear and tear. Paralysis eats my days. My emotions, pruned to cope with the new situation, need time to grow back. In 1976 an experienced journalist wrote me a letter with a passage that saved my life: "And just one more thing: don't let yourself be put under pressure of deadlines, not by anyone at any price. Write? — yes, try out a lot of things. But publish little. Be able to wait. Wait until what you write has sufficient 'bulk' so that it can't be ravaged. The capitalist market is a slaughterhouse. And just leave 'misunderstandings' to lie fallow, don't pick them up. You can't win. You'll only go under, and they'll have their harvest."

The pain has receded. Eighteen years have passed. For the last three days I've been pushing scraps of papers full of notes across my desk, reading old letters, reviews, and diaries, ripping up and burning a pile of paper ballast. I want to report on that era in simple sentences, but paralysis again sets in, keeping me from writing the first line. The moment I try, nausea overcomes me. Nausea spreads throughout my body. There's only one way to deal with the nausea: write the first sentence, and after the first the second, and after the second the third, without stopping, and after the first page I'll know how to go on.

It goes on in the hallway of a house on flat land. A friend calls. How are you? she asks. I don't know, I answer truthfully, I guess I'm depressed. That must have been the end of 1976. In the spring of 1976 the first meeting of women writers took place in Munich. Christa Reinig, Gisela V. Wysocki, Ursula Krechel, Monika Sperr, Luisa Francia, among others, participated. We were all seated together at one table. Today such a thing can't even be imagined. *Shedding* had already sold forty-four thousand copies. I can't remember ever having applied the word *depression* to describe my state of mind. Shortly after the above mentioned call I am phoned twice more. Another friend inquires politely how I feel. She has heard I wasn't doing too well. What makes you think that? I ask. Oh, somebody recently said something in some restaurant. An acquaintance calls. I heard you're depressed? she asks, without beating around the bush. Her voice sounds satisfied. She's one of those who strongly rejects *Shedding* and has taken care to distance herself from such experiments. She doesn't want to lose credibility among those in the clique for whom "art has no gender." But at the same time she'd hate to cut herself off entirely from such trials. Maybe someday it will prove to have been important to have been in that atmosphere. To her, *Shedding's* literary form is indisputable and its success worrisome. Now that she knows I'm depressed, she'll offer to reconcile. I get the creepy feeling that I am expected to pay a toll. This depression appears to fulfill an expectation. Whether it's the depression after the first book or the depression following success or the depression that's supposed to go hand in hand with writing itself, like a natural law, remains unclear.

Clarity exists in one respect: I become aware of a break. *Shedding* is a product of the spirit which I define temporally as a historical period in my life. From that moment on I would be saying: something came BEFORE *Shedding* or AFTER *Shedding*. Nothing is as it was. I am no longer an equal among peers. During the First National Congress of the new women's movement in Frankfurt in 1972 I experienced an unaccustomed euphoric feeling, thinking: I am one among thousands. The women's thing is my thing, I belong to a women's group, and for two days we have been calling ourselves Bread ♀ Roses. I'm struggling along with the other thousand here against paragraph 218.* Group members represent five different professions: a painter, a director, a film cutter, a historian, and a physical therapist. Together, we write the Women's Handbook No. 1 about abortion and contraception. My identity is secure. If anyone asks who I am, where I come from, and what I do, I answer: I'm Vera from Bread ♀ Roses.

Now my life offers me nothing in familiar form. It doesn't matter where I go, Verena Stefan is right on my heels. Not only my product, but also my opinions, my psyche, my life-style, are the object of public and private utterances. Everything is interpreted as either explicable *through* or *in spite of* the fact that I wrote *Shedding*. It

---

*The federal statute outlawing abortion.

seems to me that I have prematurely ended one life, which was to that point a sketch easily surveyed, including deviations from the social norm. I don't know of any ceremony with which I might have taken leave of my old life and bridged the new.

One part of my person has been standing for years in that hallway, like a statue listening to the voices reacting to *Shedding*. *So, you've written a book? What in the world made you think of doing something like that? What a good thing that somebody finally wrote about* THAT. *It has nothing to do with literature; it's nothing but confessional babble. The author is apparently deeply disturbed. Obstinate, she holds her nose in the air. My dear Ms. Stefan, I'm putting together an anthology, I'd like to feature you in the weekend edition, you're not in the book review section. Do you believe that a person lives better alone? Is being alone flight or freedom? She must have a palsied soul. The way she goes about it, yeah, it's just too much for me. That's too radical for me. After all, men are people too. Finally I have the right arguments in black and white! I carry your book in my purse, everywhere I go. A neurotic author who writes about her nervous inner life. This author has succeeded in breaking out of male speech and making a vocabulary useful for women. Has Verena Stefan never been able to cultivate her sensuality? But to become lesbian is also no solution. That's no lesbian book. She simply had negative experiences, but me, I've found a humane partner. She should first make a clear decision, whether she's a lesbian or not. This feminist with the radical ideas and soft, beautiful, lyrical tones, this young woman. This book is no private thing. It applies to everybody, not only members of the feminist movement. Do you believe that a society without values can survive? Send us your thoughts about life before death from the perspective of the condition of women's lives. Write quickly. Don't get too involved. Make statements clearly focused on the theme but don't exceed fifty typed lines! Be sure we have the manuscript within five days!*

For years I would answer letters personally and send polite regrets to newspapers and bookstores. Many critics — sociologists, women in German studies, feminists — pronounced *Shedding* the bible of the women's movement, a book with which all women can identify, a symbol, a cult manual. All concepts having to do with collective action, collective beliefs. *Shedding* is in fact the offspring of a collective political process. My first published words appeared under a group signature. Like everyone else, we too were saying back then: The Personal Is Political. The oppressed were no longer exclusively other people, the exploited working class and inhabitants of the so-called third world, but also us women. Books came out of the left and women's movements in which a single voice at last said "I." It was politically legitimate, and even a text consigned to the world of belles lettres appeared within the framework of the permitted. But who permitted? And who forbade? In that transitional situation many of us, with decreasing frequency, engaged in bitter verbal battle with our comrades, insisting that women were not a secondary contradiction but, rather, the salt of the earth. We gave ourselves permission to analyze from our own point of view the state of the female nation and to define it anew. Big Brother did not stop superintending us, from outside and inside our heads. Is it good enough, compared to the Great Tradition, Great Literature, Fine Art? The criteria and hurdles remained.

The work with Bread ♀ Roses launched my personal writing process. The group supported me in that, at first. I felt honored. Many were ten and more years older than me, and some of the artists had made names for themselves in their professions well before the women's movement came along. They could look back on phases of productivity and despair, of which I had no idea. They had years behind them in which they were well-known and other years in which they found themselves placed on the back burner. They talked among themselves, coming from the depths of the creative process. I was caught up in personal political action that I wanted to put into literary form. I remember how one of them asked me: When you're depressed, *what do you do then?* Several of us were sitting together on the upper deck of a tourist steamship in Berlin and were gliding from the Paul-Lincke Ufer to Glienicke. The light was bright and burning hot. The meadows on either side of the canal held their moist shadowy branches along the shore line. The question seemed empty to me, without any contour to hold onto, like the eyes of the woman who asked it. As she spoke, she turned her head to look at me. In that twist I read a particular expectation. Then another woman gave me an expectant look. Who was I that they should ask me something like that? They knew I wanted to write a book. But was that sufficient to make me one of them? I was terribly frightened; I didn't know the answer. Did I reply, "I don't know if I've ever been depressed"? I found myself on another planet because I didn't know. Or because I had been using another word for it. Or because I thought I could avoid depression by being young, quick, and wakeful. We were sitting on the open deck and squinting our eyes until they almost disappeared. It seemed to me that the other two had been spending the entire day talking about depression, about the experience each had had with it, exchanging prescriptions and maneuvers. They had hoped I would know a trick they didn't.

The artists complained that their own work came up short. Politics devours everything, they said. Art and politics! Art or politics! Art as politics! That's how it went, back and forth. The painters fought about who belonged to the better or worse school. Naturalism, Socialist realism, placating, innovative, avant-garde, surrealistic! flew through the air, as calls to arms or curses. As the group was beginning to dissolve, I inscribed myself by writing between the fractions and gradually against the remnants of group consensus. I composed the foreword to *Shedding* at the last minute, without looking left or right, without consulting the others. These two pages mark the birth of my own process of authorial individuation.

In 1974, as I was writing *Shedding*, I traveled for three months in the United States and Mexico. I stood in a Berkeley women's bookstore and, with my head slung low, swept along each and every shelf. Three thousand titles by women authors were standing there. In Germany at that time we had not a single women's bookstore and not a single feminist press. From the loudspeaker twirled "Lavender Jane Loves Women," and *Rubyfruit Jungle* and *Riverfinger Women* were that summer's hits. Judy Grahn showed me her long poem *A Woman Is Talking to Death*. She passed her hand along the book's spine and said with pride, "This time we not only did the text by ourselves but also the jacket and illustrations!"

Did the book already exist, the one I wanted to write? It didn't. Did I already know then what I wanted to write? Repeatedly over several months I read the same three books: *To the Lighthouse*, *The Bell Jar*, and *Flying*. I couldn't put a name to my own writing. I was concerned with THE truth, of that I'm sure. I was obsessed with stating THE truth. That made me frank, willing to take risks. Couples on the Left seemed thoroughly hypocritical to me, their behavior in stark contrast to revolutionary ideals. In my own voice I wrote a book to analyze in razor-sharp detail the incongruities in these relationships; I was liberal with prescriptions for action. Slowing things down, I dissected what seemed a hypocritical relationship into minute acts, separating them into individual movements and parts of a movement, into gestures and mannerisms. Close-ups, meetings in slow motion. What did this process reveal? The details contained as much mendacity as the broad lines of the relationship.

At the same time my intoxication with the truth allowed me to be effusive and inexact in my descriptions of the possible, of lesbian love. Looking back, I can wish I had had an editor who might have told me, "Wait with your descriptions of nature or of lesbian love and lesbian bodies until you know more about the one and the other and have become more experienced a writer." But I was frightfully impatient. I was so completely preoccupied with the desire to say everything I had to say that I was totally in the grip of that feeling—let it all out. No one could have put the brakes on me, really. Inspiration and support came to me twice, from my female lover at that time and a male employee in a major publishing house. There was no editor for this book. It was zero hour. Each woman was discovering herself as an author, a publisher, a producer.

For the length of one stretched instant we could still think we were all equal. Wanting our own feminist press proved to be a binding political interest. *Shedding* created factions, infighting, pigeonholing. The women's movement put in a claim for *its* product, *its* author. Readers, friends, enemies, publishers' readers, academics, colleagues, other artists, organizers of cultural events, reviewers, bookstore owners, journalists, and publishers* took notice, considering precisely how the author represented the movement. Which feminist faction, which literary direction, did she support? The women's movement split into various camps: Are you for or against its status as literature? its lesbianism? All my relationships became hostage to this. *Oh, so that's Verena? What! You know Verena Stefan?* Success corrupted all associations: *Why her and not me?*

Germany is a small country, and in the women's movement everybody knows everybody else. We all watched one another. Just as on the bourgeois literary scene, so in feminist literary circles, a point system of judgment declared *right* or *wrong, better* or *worse,* as it served one's literary career to call the shots.

From time to time I receive letters from entire school classes: Dear Verena, we were just assigned your book *Shedding.* At readings those newly turned thirty ask me, Are you still a women's movement author? and add without pausing and with an embarrassed smile, But what is it anyway, *the* movement?

Between 1975 and 1978 I did three readings of *Shedding.* Ten years later I would step willingly up to the podium, turn on the lamp, and read unpublished stories, sometimes for ten to thirty listeners. The organizers assumed that my name continued to have enough pull

---

*Translator's note: All nouns are in the feminine in the original German.

and then put on long faces. Following my initial effusiveness, *wanting and having to say it all,* and after the exaggerated response of the media, I embarked on an effort to simplify. Always less, always scantier, without commentary. Only one thing counted: the craft of writing. On the first lecture tour I set out with only a single story. It was called "White Crocodiles." Since then it's been translated into Japanese and has appeared in a German newspaper. No publisher wanted to bring it out in book form. I am especially partial to the story because with it I, the author, found myself taking on another shape. I could sit down and write a story.

After *Shedding* I wrote a second, third, and fourth book and am presently working on the fifth. I translated three books. My book of poems, *With Feet with Wings,* sold eight thousand copies and was never critiqued nor reissued because *poetry doesn't sell.* The remainders of the German translations of *Dream of a Common Language* and *Lesbian Peoples* are going for practically nothing because *they don't sell.* Where are the readers of these books? Twenty years ago we stood behind the Dream of a Common Language—we, the feminist publishers who today remainder these books, along with the authors who fought for such books.

During the Fifth International Feminist Book Fair in Amsterdam in 1992, I took part in two workshops, the first called "Censorship and Lesbian Writing." Censorship has many faces. I spoke about internal censorship. Success breeds it. So do expectations and disappointments. If a writer wants to go on writing, she's got to forget all the interpretations, everything that's been said or written about her style, literary talents and deficits, her appearance, her sexual preferences, her themes, her public appearances, and her politics. She's got to forget what other eyes see as correct or incorrect. She mustn't think that with the next book, too, reactions will be either "I'm so enthusiastic / so frustrated" or that literary criticism means above all finding fault. Only when she no longer hears these voices inside her can she find her own way to that unruly place from which her unique voice can proceed. If she's often been interpreted, if she's raised great expectations and provoked major disappointment with her first book, it means she's going to have to try even harder to forget, if she wants to write another book. The status of her first book is inexorably fixed and past, the moment when you didn't yet know what effect it would have, how it would be interpreted, classified, cited. As soon as your product hits the market, it's common property. What you've welded together will be taken apart. It will be reviewed, and with the re-view another reality succeeds your own. How very much on target is the professional jargon! A book is exposed. It will be expedited / extradited, and after distribution / extradition re-view follows.

I will never forget that writers meeting that took place in 1988 during the feminist book fair in Montreal, when an author, arriving slightly late, stood rooted to the threshold, gaping as she beheld the overflowing room. Oh, she said, I had no idea that there were so many of us. I had the impression that only the hardened form of the author, namely the book, was represented at this fair, as though the writers, the *silent voices*, weren't here at all!

It appears that, today, a woman writer needs not only a room of her own but also a common room. After all, feminist and lesbian presses manage to exist only because we continue writing, indefatigably. Authors open up, speaking from the heart of their creation, when no publishers, readers, or critics are around.

We've got bosses again in the women's movement, someone says; there are authorities who want to tell us what we should write about and how we should write.

Did your publisher also ask you to write detective fiction, since short stories don't sell?

Do your publishers stand up for you, or do they let you down? Who believes in you if your silence lasts for years or if you need ten years to write a book?

Women authors ask one another: Do you sleep well one night and the next badly? And what about alcohol? Do you get an advance? Do they give you a record of your royalties? Do you read your reviews? Are you living with your lover? Does she like the author part of you? Is she jealous of your writing? Is she proud of you?

Authors ask one another: What do you do when you're in the spotlight and your lover feels neglected, pushed aside? They ask one another: If you don't make it, *then what will you do*?

As I neared completion of *Literally Dreaming*, the inner cacophony had nearly ceased. A Mohawk Indian, a healer and painter, came to visit. She was on a European tour and shared her knowledge in personal counseling sessions and ceremonies. We talked about an artist's work and about the public. "The ebb and flow of voices has receded into the distance," I said to close the conversation. "And I can't yet remember them." The Mohawk told me, "It's in your own hands. You can decide what's more important to you—to please the public or to write what moves your heart."

I sat down and wrote what moved my heart. I wrote thirty pages about flowers, rocks, a campfire, marmalade, the seasons; about the rare sight of a heron where an entire colony used to exist; about the importance of a single blossom or a small garden in the country which contains the expansiveness, and the space and the wild, uncultivated surfaces. These thirty leaves transformed the manuscript. As I read them, I realized I'd arrived at the basic form of the verb. This has been barely understood by readers. It doesn't meet expectations, the zeitgeist, political ideology. Women have just barely learned to say "I," readers want heroines who march with a loud and strong I! They don't want a female *I* to be as important as, or at least not more important than, a plant:

> Watching the color slowly drawing back out of the red digitalis thimbles under the apple tree, how the plants stand there grown high, gradually paling, as one after the other of the blooms with the leopard pattern in the chalice fade, before they begin to wilt.

What I am describing here is a kind of sharing, a possible communication. The plant is not an object to be analyzed by a human ego. I am describing a process in which the plant changes with the evolution of the seasons and I take part in this process at the same time. The chosen verbal form allows the reader to share in this process, not from a distance, not separate from it.

Eighteen years ago I began to live a double life. Like many other lesbians I moved to the country because I was dreaming of living firsthand. In the dream appeared friends, houses and gardens, she-dogs and cats, cultural events and ritual celebrations, love of trees and plants, the fear of walking alone in a forest and the longing, without a path, without a watch, to meander out-of-doors, also the longing to take my own life in hand and to form it. Some of these dream fragments have become reality; some have failed. Why? Crises in relationships, separations, too much physical labor, financial problems. Life itself is fragile and at heart endangered like the single heron, the single blossom. Everything appears to last no more than an hour:

> . . . but now I just wanted to sit there for an hour and pick berries and in the hour of the sun to believe in the belief that was returning, to believe in having something in common sometimes, two companion lovers in the country and others around them, what is that.

The conflict between culture and nature, between the wilderness and civilization, between body and soul, seems to have no mediation. Many who live in the country behave in an arrogant manner vis-à-vis intellectual, urban life, and many city women persist in their arrogant superiority over agrarian living, which they understand as merely recreational. I have lived in the country for eighteen years and have visited the city regularly, to go to the movies, the women's bookstores, the lesbian bars, to visit friends and attend urban activities; now I'm moving back to the city for a few years.

Among reactions to *Literally Dreaming* were raging explosions against an author who loves nature and describes it in detail, and in whose world only women live. Nothing sensational happens; there's no action, no sex scenes, no struggle against men. No well-trained, sharp-shooting heroines. This time I haven't shown my readers when to go into screaming fits of rage, nor have I given them anyone with whom they should identify. For a readership used to lesbian mysteries, that's bland fare.

The land, the earth, the natural world, are, even in the feminist community, the last outpost, the inferior, the despised. There is hardly a theme that the women's movement hasn't confronted. The theme "women and nature" has been avoided in Germany. A liberation movement that fails to clarify our relationship to earth has sapped its energy before it even begins.

"To Write in the Country" was the name of the second workshop at which I participated during the Fifth International Feminist Book Fair, together with Miriam Tlali from South Africa and Olive Senior from Jamaica. When I talk about nature in foreign countries, I realize how much easier it is than to broach the subject in Germany. In foreign countries it isn't like a red flag to a bull. In Germany dealings with the subject undergo a special sort of censorship. The fascist past and the language of Nazi propaganda weigh upon us even today. My mentioning that, in Germany, the words *blood* and *soil* are taboo, because the fascist slogan *Blut-und-Boden* still carries weight, shocks my foreign colleagues. They can't imagine having to write without the words *blood* or *soil*.

The most interesting aspect of the workshop was the report by three authors who, despite coming from very different cultures, unanimously agreed that the dominant opinion always valued city over country living. The agrarian is the marginalized; the city is defined as central. But unlike myself, Miriam Tlali and Olive Senior were able to report on traditions of myth and magic, tales and customs carried forward, and were able to build on their mothers' and grandmothers' stories. Mythology, spirituality, magic, women's knowledge of healing, are still suspect to many factions in the German women's movement; they are not political themes. Each of these concepts triggers ideological debates. A person who identifies with nature is tagged unrealistic, biologistic, backward. Those feminists who reside as far as possible from the soil consider themselves cleverer, more realistic, more progressive, and more politically savvy than others.

Literally Dreaming honors *In Search of Our Mothers' Gardens,* in which desire and aesthetics meet in daily life and revere mother nature while reminding us just how much destruction has already taken place.

At the close of *Literally Dreaming* I have reached the edge of the forest. I am leaving the cultivated aesthetic, the civilized, the goal oriented, the utilitarian, behind. The she-dog reminds me that another aesthetic exists. The word *aesthetic* comes from the Greek and meant originally a hunting trail, or to follow a scent. That is the opposite of fearing the woods, the forest; it means, like Artemis, *to go in on no trail . . . simply, out of love.* A demand every bit as radical as taking back the streets at night.

My books are corporeal books. *Shedding* concerns the female and the male, and the female and the female bodies.

The poems concern female animals and female humans and other terrestrial bodies like trees or moors and temples whose forms reflect a female-bodied architecture.

In *Literally Dreaming* I deal with terrestrial bodies: wood, flowers, animals, lesbians, and materials like cement, mortar, brick, plaster, and paper.

My latest book, *Times Have Been Good,* deals mainly with my mother's body and her corporeal world, the bodies of the daughter and the mother, and with taking leave of the body through death.

Now I am writing about adolescent girls as heroines. I'm going with them into the forest, the wilderness, into the great untamed: into a physical female freedom.

Translated from the German by
Tobe Levin

Afterword

Verena Stefan, a celebrity critical of stardom, was born in 1947 in Switzerland, of a Swiss mother and Sudeten German father. Her two brothers, years older, had been born before the war. In 1968 Verena left her hometown of Bern for West Berlin, where, after concluding her training as a physical therapist, she cofounded Bread ♀ Roses, a women's group, in 1972. *Shedding* appeared in 1975, then a volume of poems, *Mit Füssen Mit Flügeln* (With Feet with Wings), in 1980. Together with Gabriele Meixner, Stefan translated into German Adrienne Rich's *Dream of a Common Language* (1982) followed by Monique Wittig and Sande Zweig's *Brouillon pour un dictionnaire des amantes* (1983). She has published essays, taught women's studies at various institutes, and, in 1977, the county of her birth honored her with a prestigious award, the Ehrengabe des Kantons Bern. But most important, she has been "living the vita" and "arriving in her story," as *Literally Dreaming's* opening and closing chapters put it. *Times Have Been Good (Es ist Reich gewesen)*, the title of her latest volume (1993), honors her mother, a person who was dedicated to her craft and wrote constantly but, like so many other women, endured the silence of never being published. In 1975, however, the diary writer's daughter went public.

"Dear Frau Stefan," wrote Renée Watkins, of the University of Massachusetts, in 1989, "Have you thought recently about bringing out another English language edition of *Shedding*? I feel that, especially now, many are longing for the honesty of the women's movement of the seventies. At least, that's my case."[1] Apparently so. Witness the popularity of Susan Faludi's *Backlash* (1991) and Marilyn

French's *The War against Women* (1992), each of which, despite feminist gains, fevers with the virus of a misogyny that is undeniably active and lethal. Or, even more to the point, we should note William Morrow's resuscitation of Shulamith Firestone's *The Dialectic of Sex* (1970; 1993), with Ingrid Bengis's *Combat in the Erogenous Zone* (1970; 1992) similarly revived. Bengis's text, like Stefan's, targets sexuality as the primary locus of women's oppression, and all three 1970s documents share the then revolutionary insight of a female sex-class. It appears that the time is ripe for a reexamination of that concept.

In 1974, however, it was a male Socialist publisher, Trikont, which provided office space to an eight-woman editorial group that accepted *Shedding* from its unknown author. The rest, as they say, is history. With no advertising or attention from a media establishment systematically disdainful or ignorant of women's work,[2] the modest volume of "autobiographical sketches, poems dreams and analyses" (the German subtitle) sold out its first print run, 3000 copies, within two months. As in the case of Rita Mae Brown's novel *Rubyfruit Jungle*, word of mouth hailed the book, which by the end of 1977 had total sales of more than 150,000. Verena's reinvestments in the collective, Frauenoffensive, facilitated its independence from the parent house, and the best-seller has continued to flourish on the backlist. To the present, 300,000 German copies, plus translations into seven European languages and Japanese, have been eagerly plucked from bookstore shelves.

Reviews began appearing in the fall of 1975, followed by longer articles and radio spots. University lecturers took notice, one comparing the book's popularity to that of Goethe's *Werther*. Or, as Angelika Bammer puts it, "*Shedding* was the feminist equivalent to what Mao's 'little red book' had been to the leftist student movement several years earlier." It appears to have had a profound effect "on the development of West German women's [writing] . . . set[ting] in motion a wave of . . . *Identifikationsliteratur* (identification literature)" (68). Stefan's text also stages a meeting of two related literary forms, the bildungsroman and the "new subjectivity," an autobiographical mix of reportage and fiction characteristic of German narrative in the 1970s (Frieden 304–5). Madeleine Marti places Stefan's work in the context of (West) German lesbian writing, concluding her study *Hinterlegte Botschaften: Die Darstellung lesbischer Frauen in der deutschsprachigen Literatur seit 1945* (Closeted Tidings: The Representation of Lesbians in German Literature since 1945) with the comment: "The decisive moment in the representation of lesbians occurred in the seventies, with differentiation following in the eighties. This can be shown by means of publication figures, themes, and content. . . . Whereas the number of lesbian narratives increased threefold from five in the fifties and sixties to fifteen in the seventies, figures soared in the eighties to about 130." And she adds, "Forging the path was Verena Stefan's *Shedding*, the pioneer whose first-person narrator encoded the shift from heterosexual to lesbian, [initiating] the emphasis on male accountability which dominated texts of the seventies (Moosdorf, Reinig, Stefan, Stenten, Schröder)" (382–3; my translation).

In the intervening years feminist standpoints have evolved which are skeptical of *Shedding*'s emphases on women's difference, their invisibility, and consequent search for identity as well as the implied claim of universal sisterhood. In "Alterity-Marginality-Difference: On Inventing Places for Women" Gisela Brinker-Gabler reviews a number of these "recent studies [that] criticize any totalizing or globalizing gesture within feminist theories, parallel to the poststructuralist critique of the unified subject. . . . [Unwilling to accept] the coherence of the category known as 'women,' [they counterpose] cultural modalities (Hull/Scott/Smith, Anzaldùa/Moraga, Mohanty/Russo/Torres) [or] the multiplicity of social and political intersections in which 'gender' is produced (Scott, Riley)" (238). Such thinking clearly calls Stefan's vision into question. But other influential theorists—Brinker-Gabler refers to Nancy Miller and Tania Modelski—point to "the deconstruction of identity [as] a luxury that women, who have never *had* anything other than a negative or marginal identity, cannot afford." A useful strategy, Brinker-Gabler suggests, is to proceed "as if" and to apply Gayatri Spivak's "strategic essentialism" (239), "taking both universalization and particularity as provisional" (243). Stefan's reliance on a gyrating process, flowing from the narrative focus on one individual to analyses of women's oppression and back again to the protagonist, can be understood in the light of this theory.

But what is *gyrating*? I use this term to describe levels of discourse, as the text leaps from formulations fit for demonstration banners to autobiographical, subjective uses of metaphor and symbols. The prose thereby personalizes the political by giving the masses a biography. For instance, when the narrator asserts, in italics, *"Sexism runs deeper than racism than class struggle,"* she has become a street-corner radical, addressing specifically the male (or male-minded) German leftist of the early 1970s who denies this, preferring instead to label women's precise disadvantage a "secondary contradiction" that, from the Marxist perspective, will wither away under socialist rule. Dave, a black male lover, stands for this "most revolutionary of comrades," reinforcing through his advocacy of "Cleaver and Malcolm X" an unacceptable place for women, one that refuses to theorize female sexuality. Stefan's implied reader knows that Malcolm X espoused a form of black Muslim culture stressing "modesty," and Cleaver's taxonomy of racism's effects gave us the white male "Omnipotent Administrator," with his debilitated female on a pedestal, and the black male "Supermasculine Menial," with an amazon as his feminine counterpart. Though these are descriptive, not prescriptive, labels, a notorious chapter in *Soul on Ice* advocates raping white women. Dave, of course, is not a rapist. Quite the contrary. Yet he is portrayed as being "much more in touch with his body than most whites and was convinced that their sensuality had atrophied." Is this description a lapse into political incorrectness, flirtation with a reprehensible stereotype?

Yet Dave does not enjoy superior endowment. Instead, the personal drama contradicts political posturing, for he "gets angry" when "his penis slips out," a slippage that happens with Samuel, too, and consigns his female partner to her traditional compensatory role: "I try very hard to position myself correctly until he gets his orgasm." Dave's political self-image, identifying with sexual prowess, is shown to rest, like similar claims by white men, on female complicity, a subservience shared by multiethnic women: "The millenial genealogy in which woman upon woman, head bowed, filled with compassion, bends over a man of stone, is made up of black white yellow brown men and women." As the Combahee River Collective has written: We will fight with our men over sexism. Stefan endorses this female commonality.

Exhibiting a militancy not unlike many black feminist theorists defying patriarchal norms, Stefan's protagonist makes commitment the very condition of her art. The protagonist takes up writing as a result of her participation in the women's movement, publishing *for* the movement. Hers is a literature of praxis, as Jean-Paul Sartre has defined it, "one which attempts an active role in mediating between the world and [our] capacity to change it" (in Caute 46).

By any standards, then, *Shedding* can be viewed as a unique phenomenon in German literary history and as significant for women's publishing. Although the author might have transferred her text to an enterprise with greater media influence and increased advertising budget, she chose not to, explaining in her afterword to the eleventh edition in 1977: "My decision to go with a feminist house was deliberate; I wanted to support this sort of autonomous movement institution" (126). The book was born of political intent: "Writing had always offered one possible medium [for activism]," Stefan notes, "but . . . remained dormant for years. The decision to write and to publish grew out of my work with Bread ♀ Roses, in part with the members' encouragement and support" (1977, 125).

Bread ♀ Roses, active between 1972 and 1974, whose projects *Shedding* mentions, offered counseling services, demonstrated for reform of paragraph 218 (outlawing abortion), and published *Frauenhandbuch Nr. 1* (The First Women's Handbook) on abortion, contraception, and female anatomy and sexuality, whose introduction, which Stefan helped to draft, states: "Our attempt to analyze the sexual and social relations forcing us to take whatever, mainly inadequate, contraceptive measures are available, should give us a clearer understanding of women's sexual oppression and mutilation. These we intend to abolish" (2; my translation). In theory, then, in 1972 the female body was already at the heart of German feminism.

At mid-decade, when Stefan's slim volume appeared, continuing invitations to foreign (especially Turkish) laborers (*Gastarbeiter*) testified to the expanding West German economy; unemployment was relatively low, and, as elsewhere, the women's movement was searching for a voice, defining itself as autonomous. As Lillian Faderman argues in *Odd Girls and Twilight Lovers: A History of Lesbian Life in Twentieth-Century America* (1991), prosperity creates the circumstances in which women may achieve economic independence, thus making possible the flowering of lesbian culture. West Germany's increasing affluence may therefore have contributed to the profound impact of *Shedding* on educated young women readers, for whom its radical appeal seemed within the limits of what could be realistically imagined. Its autobiographical narrator proposes a politics of lesbian identity, not unlike Adrienne Rich's "lesbian continuum," using metaphors and imagery drawn largely from nature, while the text departs from orthodox spelling and orthography, which thematize language itself. Stefan, whose protagonist painfully sheds her conditioning by and dependence on men by groping toward a sexual idiom not contaminated by the mutilating gaze of males, spoke even to the most politically critical issues, as Socialist-feminist Gabriele Goettle notes: "Women's distancing themselves from men was and is a precondition for their own

exploration of possibilities, needs, analyses and politics, for learning, theory and praxis" (5).

We can better understand why the most resonant text, fiction or
nonfiction, to emerge during the early years of the current wave was
a lesbian book—the first in that nation's literary history to affirm
lesbianism as a choice (Marti 141)—once we look more closely at
German history. "While German feminists may at times seem very
familiar [to Americans], they differ from their Anglo-American
counterparts in their emphasis on women's difference from men,"
wrote Atina Grossman and Sara Lennox in 1987 in the *Women's
Review of Books*. Discussing the 1984 anthology *German Feminism:
Readings in Politics and Literature*, they note that "none of the selec-
tions plot strategies for entry into male arenas and most evince a
bitter suspicion of mainstream institutions. No essay projects any
hope for more egalitarian intimate relations between the sexes, and
heterosexual eroticism is treated only with anger and bitterness"
(15). This emphasis on women's difference from men characterized
the reception of *Shedding*.

Angelika Bammer concurs. Reminding us that in 1975 Alice
Schwarzer published her best-selling *Der "kleine Unterschied" und
seine großen Folgen: Frauen über sich. Beginn einer Befreiung* (The Minor
Difference and Its Major Consequences: Women Speaking Out about
Themselves. First Steps Toward Liberation),[3] which sold out seven
printings in the first year, she notes, "While Stefan's approach was
literary and Schwarzer's sociological, the substantive focus of their
texts was virtually identical: women's sexual oppression at the hands
of men. With the publication of these two books West German
feminism moved from what had begun and was then still perceived
as a more or less isolated and marginal movement into the larger
public sphere" (67).

The movement's origins further explain a separatist drive in
German feminism. Hilke Schlaeger points out that, in significant
contrast to U.S. activists, Germans did not come to realize discrimi-
nation of their sex by first participating in another liberation movement, for example, as abolitionists or civil rights workers. Rather, the
movers and shakers in the late 1960s had at first worked closely with
male fellow students, sharing leftist goals—for autonomy and against
authoritarian structures. But, Schlaeger notes, "As in every other
country . . . [leftist] women typed pamphlets . . . written by men,
brewed coffee to keep the men awake, and comforted their comrades
after a day's work with the same thing women have always used to

comfort tired warriors—their sexuality" (62). In September 1968 future filmmaker Helke Sander stood before an assembly of radicals at the University of Frankfurt and warned that, if women's expectations continued to be ignored, a power struggle would ensue, and, indeed, acrimonious splits followed. As Edith Hoshino Altbach notes:

> To the outside observer, the alienation of feminists from the left seems more complete in West Germany than in the United States. . . . The phrase "*autonomous* women's movement" is used constantly, apparently to signal a distinction from the more traditional marxist-leninist groups. An example of this alienation can be found in the call for papers for the first Summer University for Women at the Free University of Berlin in 1976 which welcomed all women "except those who, under the cloak of a commitment to women, seek to sell an ideology which relegates the oppression of women to a secondary or subordinate status." (10–11)

Or, as Schlaeger sees it, "the worst enemy is on the left": "Every leftist woman is suspected of harboring a male comrade within herself" (63).[4] It is therefore understandable that the first broad-based spectacle that the contemporary movement both launched and was launched by concerned women's difference. In 1971, having lived for a number of years in France, journalist Alice Schwarzer duplicated the Gallic self-accusation campaign under the motto *I Have Had an Abortion.* The female body thus became the lightning rod of movement activism.

By means of flashbacks, internal monologues, diary fragments, and anecdotes, each of *Shedding's* four chapters principally concerns differing stages en route to psychosomatic integrity. "Shadow Skin," by far the longest, dramatizes growing up to be a man's woman; "Withdrawal Symptoms" traces attempts to break out of dependence on men; "State of Emergency" involves learning to love women and facing the knife edge of alienation; while the "Gourd Woman" moves closer to self-love. "Shadow Skin" differs from the rest in that it deals with a shared female reality; in the remaining three chapters a pioneer steps out of the ranks.[5]

Stefan has blazed the trail toward a number of goals. One question preoccupying feminist Germanists since the mid-1970s has been Silvia Bovenschen's, "Is there a feminine aesthetic?" Stefan's linking ideology to aesthetics suggests that belles lettres can function as an instrument of movement agitation. Stefan was on to something truly potent by expressing her feminist politics in the form of a mixed literary genre. And even if the autobiographical elements in *Shedding* were chosen for effect, as the author noted in an early interview, it would appear that narrative opened theory to the broadest reading public. The illusion of identification with a courageous heroine, in the old-fashioned sense of the term, may be a key to the efficacy of storytelling as an organizing tool. It certainly takes seriously the claim that "the personal is political," pouring that idea into aesthetic molds.

The feminist theories Stefan weaves into her textual fabric are numerous, but we need only look at the first few pages to see how narrative and theory intertwine in *Shedding*. Opening the story is a "cascade of greening birches," a tactile and visual metaphor (the technical term is *synesthesia*) which immediately invokes the protagonist's complaint, expressed later in terms of colonization, that a girl's taming expropriates her body and marks "the onset of numbness." That nature, rather than another person, should catalyze a sensual awakening is both an aspect of plot and theme, for heterosexual relationships fall short in precisely this respect: where patriarchy has taught a woman to seek her sensual fulfillment—in bed with a man—the narrator finds that planes crash, lions roar, instruments slide out. Nature succeeds where human beings fail.

The book's second scene then takes on the theme of women's vulnerability to male assault on the streets and ties it brilliantly to alienation from the female body proceeding from other causes, all of which, however, relate to male supremacy. The young woman laden with groceries finds herself accosted and humiliated by two couples at a sidewalk café who harass her with the line "What knockers!" Once safely away from public space and in her own apartment, the irritated shopper refers to her breasts as "sun-filled gourds," anticipating the story's end. Nonetheless, the male world and its women's auxiliary succeed in demeaning a female simply by referring to her femaleness. The taunt "What happened to your boobs?" hurts so much because the narrator's body "did not measure up to standards." "It didn't have a good figure," she says. Alienation is apparent in the nonpossessive, impersonal pronoun *it*.

Ample research on eating disorders and beauty myths confirms that few women believe their physique measures up. That "it all related to my body," that is, the compulsion to have had heterosexual experience to win men's "approval," draws a thread through the story's four inaugural scenes. In the first, the cascading birches invoke both lack of and heightened feeling, a theme made more explicit in the third vignette, in which a bathing child remembers the intensity of "pores" and "fibers . . . tingling" with an overwhelming newness. Instead of delighting in itself, in the second and fourth scenes the body, in public and in private, hurts. "There was the pain" the narrator claims in the very act of being penetrated. Pain weds the street and the bed.

Is "genital solemnity," the use of coitus as a substitute for intimacy, to blame for this? Would a "private revolution," women taking their own destinies in hand, attenuate the painful or numbing effects of heterosexual intimacy and public assault? In "Withdrawal Symptoms" the theoretician and dramatist blend axiom and personal lyric to explore this theme in a manner that illustrates the feminist writer's political aesthetic:

> [Samuel] does not want to accept the fact that copulation has to be put aside for a time if it is to be experienced anew and given a different priority. "I can't do without it!" he claims.
> Without a vagina? Without a woman? Without people?

A program of temporary chastity, stated as a dry directive, elicits a "live," dramatic rejoinder. Samuel speaks, rejecting the postulate but also calling attention to its negativity. For what is to replace the act? What narrative details or gestures fill out the kind of interaction the protagonist envisions?

> If I could look into his eyes *just to look into his eyes!*
> If I could caress him *just to caress him!*
> If I could kiss him *just to kiss him!*
> ....
> If we would want to see each other, in order to find each other,
> What a revolution!
> Down with copulation!

The poem takes us to a demonstration—written on the banner is a parody of anticapitalist slogans—and it also spells out a political purpose. At issue is the concept of "foreplay." Why be*fore*? Before what? Male programming in sex cannot bring this woman to flower:

But
Whether I look into his eyes, caress or kiss him, our hands fail to meet, they touch only emptiness. The glances splinter the moment they meet. . . .
Orgasm has been blown up out of proportion. It has flattened sexuality. It is all that remains of sexuality. Everything else is forgotten, including the question of what an orgasm actually is and what significance it might have for human understanding.

A multiplicity of voices elides the political and personal. This prose-framed poem places an academic's cadences before and after a lyrical appeal to the reader's experience of adolescent male hands, which many might remember hoping would soon desist from their awkward explorations in the backseats of cars in the 1960s. Men's genital solemnity, theorized poetically, identifies the tyrant keeping women from expanding their undetermined sensual potential.

And yet, in terms of learning the female body, the protagonist barely goes beyond negation:

> We have learned to kiss the penis, and yet are afraid of the
> lips between our own legs.
> The hand on its way to the clitoris
> of another woman
> traverses centuries.
> It can get lost a thousand times.
> It fights its way through fragments of civilization.
> And in addition, the route it takes
> leads to a place that has no name:
> I have no clitoris.
> I have no vagina. No vulva. No pussy.
> No bust, no nipples.

The earlier assault scene recurs in this defense. "No knockers, no boobs," we might add. And no safety either. For the poet makes of the body a place unsited on a nonexistent map, "the lips between our legs [en] route . . . to a place [with] no name." Shedding means stripping ourselves of labels suited to male functions (as *vagina* = *penile sheath*). The activist artist erases the canvas.

> No places on my body . . . correspond to these . . . brutal designa-
> tions. Clitoris has nothing in common with this part of my body which

is called clitoris. . . . [Nor is it] my focal point, my life does not revolve around it. . . . [N]ot that I want to minimize its importance, it is just that I do not want to be limited again to only one part of my body.

How are women to rewrite the script? By altering their routes: "In order to find new words I will have to live differently for as many years as I have lived believing in the meaning of these terms."

In "Critical Clitoridectomy: Female Sexual Imagery and Feminist Psychoanalytic Theory" (1993) Paula Bennett argues convincingly that, in fact, uncovering clitoral symbolism has recently made it possible "to establish just how autonomous and independent of male sexual symbology" the female organ has been from the nineteenth century to the present, in Western literature, although readers have been afraid to see what was there. Those symbols "(bud, pearl, berry, seed, jewel [in Stefan, the 'blossoming labella' or former snapdragons]) . . . make [the female] the agent of her own desire, an autonomous desiring subject in her own right" (254). To Stefan, however, who lacked such pioneering guides to clitoral presence, escape from phallocratic definitions appears the more promising strategy, indeed the necessary precondition. Skewered for centuries on the rod of reductive, patriarchal thought, the woman nesting in Stefan's heroine remains cocooned. Looking not to literature but to life, the central metaphor—at times a lizard, losing leather to reveal the same form beneath, but at others an onion, which, if peeled enough, leaves nothing—is consonant with the political platform: to emphasize the female's erasure, which phallocracy achieves through reification.

In her view of *Shedding* Bammer also suggests the importance of a reading that emphasizes contradiction and the irony involved in a project so steeped in the negative.

> *Shedding* functioned as a mirror on to which women readers projected themselves. At the same time, however, it challenged the very specular economy of women's "identification literature." . . . [For] instead of providing reassurance, it produces [malaise]. . . . Neither the narrating nor the experiencing self are [sic] presented as coherent or self-evident [but are] rather . . . fragmented into many possible [intersecting, overlapping, contradictory] selves. The [reader's] desire to fix . . . an identity—to see herself as the woman in the text, for example—is thus concomitantly thwarted by the fact that the woman in the text is unable to establish her own identity, much less propose one for generic

woman. An identificatory reading is systematically disrupted . . . by a refusal of coherence on all levels: neither plot, narrative voice, tone, not even genre, remain constant. (69)

"We are who we are in the process of becoming," Bammer concludes (70). Indeed, the private upheaval signifies action. "I lead a different life, speak another language," notes the heroine. "Different," "another"—defined in opposition to a norm, woman is yet high on the liberty and danger the unknown offers. *Shedding*, an exploratory manual, testifies to feminist faith in individual efforts whose outcome, however, is yet uncertain: "Leading one single life differently is important for radically changing society as a whole, one single life led long before 'day x' (what is 'day x'?), one single life that may not bring this day about but which could bring it closer."

Of the many feminist positions taken by Stefan in *Shedding* none appears to have attracted as much attention as this coup d'état which cuts to the heart of Socialist thinking in terms of collectivities, the book's implied readers residing to an overwhelming extent in that camp. The more Left-leaning critics fear that it reproduces, rather than disrupts, the traditional division between politics and personal life. P. P. Zahl, Sigrid Weigel, and others writing in the influential *Kursbuch* 47 ("Frauen," March 1977) were reluctant to accept Stefan's point, which I see as showing the subject's dialectical relationship to social forces not to reproduce the division between public and private but, rather, to suggest that *this opposition never existed anywhere but in ideology*. This entails the rigorous interrogation of patriarchal language.

Jeanette Clausen confirms this: "Stefan recognizes that different living and different language are inextricably related" (5). And Theresa de Lauretis goes further, asserting that "the relation of experience to discourse, finally, is what is at issue in the definition of feminism" (5). Thus, if a woman is to enjoy autonomy, she needs words that do not denigrate her body. Liberation strategy calls for the dismantling of phallocratic terms. In 1993 Barbara Becker-Cantarino reaffirms that "the central problem in women's production of literature is [still] escaping from tutelage (speaking for herself as an independent individual and finding the personal idiom in which to do so)" (225; my translation). In her 1975 foreword Stefan agrees:

I kept bumping into the language at hand, word [by] word, concept [by] concept [and] all the more intensely because I was writing about sexuality. *All* the customary expressions which refer to coitus—the spoken as well as the written ones—are brutal and denigrate women (i.e., *screw, fuck, thrust, bang, stick it in*). The leftist idiom reflects the existing power structure in much the same way, though perhaps a shade more bluntly. The leftist cock enters the leftist pussy and people (merrily) screw around. But the processes themselves remain unaffected. To say *enter* instead of *penetrate* does not take issue with the fact of the matter. If a woman starts talking about her pussy, she is merely adopting the jargon of leftist men. Her vagina, her body, her true self remain to her as inaccessible as before. If she uses these expressions to talk "candidly" about her body and her sexuality, this merely means she is conforming to male attempts at overcoming sexual taboos. So when I write about heterosexuality, I . . . use the clinical terminology. It is more neutral, less offensive, further removed.

Language fails me the moment I attempt to describe new experiences. Experiences that are supposedly new cannot be considered really new if they are expressed in the same everyday idiom. Articles and books that treat the subject of sexuality without addressing the problem of language are worthless; they serve to maintain the status quo. (53)[6]

Clearly, poetry is not a luxury, to borrow Audre Lorde's expression, for it alone, in its inventiveness, escapes the familiar denigrating language. Stefan's introduction to *Frauenoffensive Journal No. 5,* "Aufständische Kultur" (Rebellious Culture), points out the cardinal relationship of script to body by quoting Hélène Cixous's dictum:

Un texte féminin ne peut pas ne pas être plus que subversif: s'il s'écrit, c'est en soulevant, volcaniquement, la vieille croute immobilière. . . . Il faut qu'elle s'écrive parce que . . . en s'écrivant, la Femme fera retour à ce corps qu'on lui a plus que confisqué, dont on a fait l'inquiétant étranger . . . cause et lieu des inhibitions. A censurer le corps on censure du même coup le souffle, la parole. . . . Ecrire, acte que "réalisera" le rapport dé-censuré de la femme à sa sexualité, à son être-femme, lui rendant access à ses propres forces. (1975, 175)

[A woman's text can't be anything less than subversive, for only a volcanic force can explode the ancient petrifying crust. . . . [And] the woman's text must be produced because writing will return woman to the female body that has suffered worse than confiscation; it has become a troubling foreigner, trigger and site of inhibitions. Censoring the body has meant cutting off the breath, the word. . . . [But] writing will create the decensored relation of woman to her sexuality, to her womanness, renewing access to her strengths.] (My translation)

At the *Treffen schreibender Frauen* (Women Authors Meeting) in Munich in 1976, Stefan used the phrase "writing with the body" ("Mit-dem-Körper-schreiben" [Brug and Hoffmann-Steltzer 122]), in apparent agreement with Cixous's attributing to narrative the function of empowerment. Hence, a double strategy, lesbian separatist living and the concomitant recording of it, characterizes Stefan's project. An early interview with Johanna Müller confirms this: "I consider myself a part of a newly evolving women's culture . . . that is, that I intend my pages to describe novel content communicated in innovative ways. And the unaccustomed content relates intimately to my life, the fact that I live with other women and describe this life among women" (my translation).

In an unpublished *arbeitspapier* (working paper) from a discussion between Stefan and Kathrin Mosler on 3 March 1976, the two elaborate: "Culture no longer elevated. Division of art from life revoked. A new way of living must precede this to bridge the chasm between the literary and the lived." Hence, Stefan and Mosler conclude, "We find our starting point in the woman writer's life, in her social circumstances, and not in literary history" (Frauenoffensive files; my translation).

This life's refusal of confinement in patriarchal categories leads to the climate of uncertainty in which *Shedding*'s heroine learns to love a sister artist, the relationship both anxiety provoking and exhilarating in its creative possibilities: "Being together demanded a great [many hours]. Our intimacies were circumspect. In the time it took for us to exchange a single kiss, I would in the past have already had intercourse and found myself standing there fully clothed and ready to depart" (in the original: "das zusammen sein forderte den raum vieler stunden") (100).

I've quoted the German here to illustrate an aspect of Stefan's linguistic experiment which is lost in translation. Among her attempts to draw our attention to language per se are defiance of orthographic rules—German nouns should be capitalized—and broken spellings. Here *zusammen sein* = *zusammensein*, being together; hers is a sardonic splitting. A more telling example are the German words for *bra* and *girdle*, *Bustenhalter* and *hüftgürtel*: "Although occasionally I got the feeling that I could occupy my whole body, I was nonetheless evicted from it piece by piece. The pride I felt at my first bra, my first girdle, my first lipstick!" When taken apart *hüft gürtel* (= girdle) underscores that part of the torso encased, while *Busten halter* consists of bosoms and container, suggesting, as one reader notes, "a truly cynical-technocratic understanding of our bodies" (Anders 120; my translation). Ricarda Schmidt explores the startling effect of such divisions (64), whose use Jeanette Clausen applauds, because: "the conventions of linguistic usage and meaning are both alienating and oppressive": "[Stefan] sees, for example, the subordination of aspects of self for a woman in patriarchal society paralleled by and reflected in the subordination of linguistic elements to one another (e.g., *Unterleib, Ehefrau, Bewußtsein*) (13)."

Stefan's natural metaphors—flowers for genitals, trees for ambience—represent a similar attempt to use language strategically, as an escape from phallocratic definitions. Although critics Ricarda Schmidt and Margret Brügmann sense danger in these traditional comparisons, asking whether it isn't playing into the hands of patriarchy to reinforce the association of woman with nature, which has disempowered females, I think not, if we understand nature as a "raw material" (Mosler 51) being reinvested with new meanings. As Schmidt herself shows in a discussion of the poem in *Shedding* which begins "I am quite sure," reference to the past can be viewed as phylogenetic, "dwelling in trees" suggesting a relation of female to nature cleansed of the will to dominate (80).

Margret Brügmann also analyzes the role of the natural in *Shedding*, contending that one might think the heroine's sojourn in northern Germany merely a reproduction of the traditional romantic split between city and country. Nonetheless, she notes, at various moments throughout the text, rural life appears both contradictory and complex (38–39). In particular when visiting Nadjenka, the narrator ponders:

> I watch her while she pares vegetables. She holds an onion in the palm of her hand. She fingers it for a few moments before peeling and slicing it. How is it that Nadjenka has the time to hold an onion in her hand long enough for the sensation of it to actually leave behind a momentary impression? There are more pressing things, time itself is more pressing, it presses continuously, there is so much to be done.
> "I don't use the same board anymore for cutting fruits and vegetables," she says, interrupting my thoughts. "Once I put my nose

to it, you wouldn't believe it, that combination of banana and onion was disgusting."

Is that important? Is it revolutionary? When will the right time have come for learning to savor aromas?

Literally Dreaming suggests that the time will not come on its own, but must be taken. The eight stories in *Literally Dreaming* dramatize the life lived differently, even as the author in *Shedding* had envisioned, independent of immediate male intervention.[7]

An additional strategic link between *Literally Dreaming* and *Shedding* may be found in the following flight of irony suggesting the complexity of its quest for change. Is this the voice of utopian idealism?

> By then I was fed up, why do it myself, why bother, I'd earn a lot of money and be able to buy what I need . . . and I need the time for the stimulation I need and the inspiration comes only when the mind is totally free and I as a free person live a totally free life and can drive anytime anywhere I want to where maybe I'll see or hear something that might inspire me, the quiet in the country at night I'd manage to put up with, but the wood business and the preserve business and the garden business, all that just keeps me away from the real arts, I thought. ("With Head and Hair," last section)

An antagonistic voice, like the one answered in the first chapter, whose narrator defends her choice of country living, takes over from the pioneer, who had indeed concerned herself with connections between the human routine and natural rhythms. The irony here, however, disarms that internalized critic, unhinging the dyads on which it is based: urban/rural, production/consumption, liberation/slavery, each term honed with a feminist edge. "[So] I thought," the narrator concludes, pulling the rug out from under her supposed preference for city, art and freedom, as opposed to the country, its sensations and constraints. Which really offers more to the artist, to the lesbian? The question is open, as suggested in the following dilemma reminiscent of Nadjenka's cutting board: "Standing with the apple in my hand under the faucet as if a film had stopped, unable to decide whether I should eat the apple with the acid rain on it or if I should rinse it off with the recycled water from some dubious processing plant."

Literally Dreaming can be seen as being linked to *Shedding*, insofar as the different life is dramatized but not idealized. Running through both books is also the red thread tying the eight tales to one another: the theme of shelters, among which are caves, homes, and books. As in *Shedding*, in which the body houses dread or pleasure, and in *Literally Dreaming*, in which it "stores" "experiences" in "[body] cells," so too does each chapter in *Literally Dreaming* reproduce a version of the shingled house serving as frontispiece.

"Living the Vita" meshes dailiness with the record of it, the curriculum vitae clearly a rickety repository for the luxurious detail offered by the school of sight or smell. "The Older the Better" reintroduces the shedding metaphor: stripping centuries of residues from walls and floors is work described as the "bodybound real [with] tangible rooms, kneading and modeling after intangible sojourns of spirit and mind." The dismantling and exploration also suggest that section in *Shedding* in which the heroine, with speculum and lamp, explores the hidden passages within her frame. In "Not a Page Left Out" a diary becomes the refuge: "She must be very lonely, too, your mother" [says the neighborwoman], "if she writes that much." In "With Head and Hair," referring to the reappearance of the goddess, the gymnasium and shower room shelter the members of a lesbian community. "And That Is the Reason" also deals with home but one snowed in, confining, ventilated only by fantasy and reading. "As Unquestioning in Daylight as in Dreams" offers the needed escape from the preceeding chapter's bindings. Under a southern sky companion lovers journey in time through the centuries of female disempowerment to the Greek origins of Western culture and then place that site in temporal perspective by evoking the sparkling points in the darkened dome: "Looking at the stars into the light that travels in relays of thousands of millenia taking thousands of years to pass through female cultures to reach us." The long view guides us into the penultimate chapter, "We Work Here," whose sheltering structure is now a temple, to become a cave in the final section. *Shedding* continues as stripping, excavating, and exploring before renovation can begin. For even on the land "what the senses could take in reach . . . [the protagonist] slowly, through many layers." But, as in *Shedding*, "firsthand sensations" gradually become perceptible.

The dustjacket of the German edition, however, refers to *Shedding* only to place any kinship under scrutiny: "Not a pamphlet, a sequel to nor a repetition of a . . . cult book, [*Literally Dreaming*] is a poetic book in an unpoetic world," claims the publisher. In fact, by 1987 times had changed for the worse. With the growing rate of German unemployment, even before reunification, hostility to foreigners and the overt expression of bias had increased. Struggles that had taken place since *Shedding* was first published included opposition to nuclear power plants and to the stationing of cruise missiles on German soil. The Chernobyl plant had nearly melted down, and U.S. starfighters persistently streaked across the skies in *Literally Dreaming*. A personal protest against the fall maneuvers in the book brings few results, suggesting that the notion of what constitutes political activity had grown more restrictive over the decade. In 1975 Verena Stefan's individualistic approach calling for a private revolution, though controversial, had also been seductive. In 1987 fragments of that personal upheaval encountered even greater skepticism.

Received by major media reviewers with great curiosity thirteen years after *Shedding, Literally Dreaming* occasioned critiques of its woman centeredness, now suspected of being insufficiently differentiated from National Socialist emphases on separate spheres. In " 'Language Is Also a Place of Struggle': The Language of Feminism and the Language of American *Germanistik*" (1993) Ruth-Ellen B. Joeres helps to explain this reaction by arguing that feminism and German studies remain "reasonably unrelatable," in part as a result of "a need in the post–World War II era either to depoliticize German language and literature"—as a counterweight to Hitler's having politicized them—"or to view the future in a sort of entrenched pessimistic light" (247).[8]

Mistrust of a lesbian's preference for rural over urban living, misread as naive idealism, characterized one strain of *Literally Dreaming*'s reception. Reviewer Beatrice Eichmann-Leutenegger repeated an earlier refrain, asking whether "the propagated female closeness to nature" isn't a trap serving patriarchal interests. Another critic accuses *Literally Dreaming* of being a voice for the "new femininity," a nonstrategy, a retreat, a dead end. But does Verena Stefan really celebrate a "New Earthmother cult" (Angela Praesent)? Does the text describe "a ghetto" set within a "deceptively idyllic nature" (Eichmann-Leutenegger)?

KL, in *Prima Donna / Berliner Frauenzeitung*, argues decisively that it does not:

> She doesn't make a paradise of nature. Flight from the city doesn't solve problems that in the country simply appear in other garb:

The starfighters and troop maneuvres that invade your own garden, poisonous pesticides and the struggle with hundreds of famished slugs, the hole in the ozone layer, nuclear reactor accidents and acid rain—it's all there. Except that you can see in the animals and plants in the countryside precisely what it is that also makes a human depressed and deeply saddened: the destruction of idylls and places of retreat. (My translation)

Nor are the eight narratives intended to prescribe a form of living; they don't preach—I suspect because the author is herself uncertain. Clausen highlights the narrator's "efforts to find ecologically correct ways to battle the snails in her garden," illustrative of "the difficulty or perhaps impossibility of living in harmony with nature in . . . late twentieth century [Germany]" (1994, 6). The newer text presents neither a fault-free world nor claims to be a blueprint for political activity. The academic voice we heard in *Shedding* has been muted. Like other postmoderns, Stefan's poetic approach to the wor(l)d privileges subjectivity and location.

Marti considers such introspection characteristic of German lesbian texts of the 1980s. Whereas coming-out stories were common in the 1970s, the 1980s featured suicide, alcohol, and separation. *Literally Dreaming,* in "And That Is the Reason," enters this tradition by dealing with depression. "Life spirits . . . slither along the walls of the soul" as both protagonists struggle to find reasons to rise, deciding that "it depends on her whether she continues to live or not." But reading offers an escape from suicidal urges. So does writing. If differentiation describes more recent German lesbian fiction, the author heroine of *Shedding,* reappearing in the second decade, espouses an aesthetic that rejects generic heavy-handedness: "What is true to the letter? . . . an old farmhouse . . . entirely covered with scale-shaped shingles, each individual . . . painted by hand, each in a different shade. Millions of shingles. . . ." *Literally Dreaming* allies liberation—the freedom of the idiosyncratic, the unduplicable—and writing within a destabilized project, as suggested by the title's wordplay: literally dreaming, the writer cannot reach a utopian goal outside the book. But the book, sheltering the lives within it, would seem to be enough.

Ultimately, the narratives stand as witness to and participant in a unique women's culture.

Once, in the restored house, with the foyer tile still loose, the window glass uneven, and the wood stove burning,[9] Verena,

Johanna Albert, and I met to talk about *Literally Dreaming*. Explaining the centrality of the basketball scene to the portrait of lesbian culture, Verena said, "It represents the intimate community of thirty-two lesbians living on the land" whose experience she encodes and gives back to its source during a reading in the text. She then moved this reading into reality by presenting just this passage at the Montreal Feminist Book Fair in 1988.

For her the supportive international environment contrasted sharply with the general tenor of mainstream critiques in the German Federal Republic. "If I had only the literature business, the critics, and not the community, I'd be in the same situation as Sylvia Plath or Ingeborg Bachmann, who killed themselves," Verena admitted. "And I understand. For a writer, if she's alone, there's no other alternative to the literary popes, all of whom are men, including the women with male minds. That makes feminist book fairs unspeakably important." Stefan misses in Germany "the level of international discussion." German critics, she notes, are inadequate sounding boards for lesbian writing's spiritual resonance. "Reading in Oslo and Montreal is so refreshing," she concluded, "because a language of magic, spirituality and complicity between woman and nature is not taboo."

Influenced by ecofeminism and the women's health movement, *Literally Dreaming* attempts to reinvest the German language with meanings drawn from international lesbian writing (Isabel Miller, Christa Reinig, Marguerite Duras, Susan Griffin). The book's controversial reception suggests that a transnational lesbian culture may not be visible from the reviewers' parochial worldview. "[West] German critics separate politics from art, art from nature, magic from politics, divisions that are deathly boring but appear to be the order of the day," Stefan explains. But *Literally Dreaming* bridges such divisions. As Elsbeth Pulver recognizes: the book presents facets of a world both "experienced and made, the lives of women in the Swabian Alps . . . who consciously reject the rigidly scheduled, the consumption-oriented, and express the desire to produce, repair, build and plant as much as possible themselves; to learn what nature can give without exploiting it; to ask lovingly and patiently, what nature needs. . . . And this not as theory but as daily life."

In a discussion pertinent to the present reception of Stefan's work, Joeres describes feminism as "look[ing] not only back, not only to the present, but think[ing] in utopian ways about the future":

Feminism will insist on rebutting the pessimism that sees no future, no possibility for change. Feminism has, for example, also challenged the negativity of poststructuralism in its questioning of the unified self. . . . Not in favor of a reification into some transcendent self, . . . it nevertheless stresses the importance of thinking about identity and position, particularly from the standpoint of those . . . just beginning to grasp their own identity as women. Feminism will speak with great optimism about the idea of multiple voices, existing in community. (253)

Inspired by a utopian hope without being captive to it, *Literally Dreaming* places these voices, this community, on location, taking the private upheaval of *Shedding* one step further. As my sister expatriate Johanna Albert told me, she celebrates *Literally Dreaming*'s transatlantic voyage because these pages represent the texture and complexity of her lesbian life in Germany, and she welcomes North American access to her European world.

As Adrienne Rich has written: "The most notable fact that culture imprints on women is the sense of our limits. The most important thing one woman can do for another is to illuminate and expand her sense of actual possibilities" (264). Both *Shedding* and *Literally Dreaming* expand the universe for women. And how necessary is this literal dreaming, back and forth, beyond patriarchy to that time before, as Stefan writes, they burned us. In defiance of male media dons, *Shedding* and *Literally Dreaming* neither evade nor obscure but, rather, compel their readers to feminist reflection through their own persistent honesty.

Tobe Levin

Notes

Thanks go to Jeanette Clausen and Karin Hermann for inspiring comments on an early draft of this essay.

1. Personal communication, Renée Watkins to Verena Stefan, 28 February 1989.

2. Women's writing in Germany has had an even steeper uphill battle for legitimacy within the critical establishment than in the United States as a result of the term *Frauenliteratur.* Literally "women's literature," the word connotes the trivial and banal characteristic of pulp. Women authors, avid to be taken seriously, would distance themselves from this label and hence from the word *woman.*

3. Schwarzer is editor-in-chief of *Emma, Ms.* magazine's German cousin, and her name is a household word. Throughout 1992 she hosted a biweekly talk show on Hessian television.

4. Hoshino Altbach traces animosity between the mainstream or "bourgeois" feminist and Socialist woman to the nineteenth and early twentieth centuries: "The leftist legend of the stab in the back it received from the new female voters during the Weimar Republic is still alive, and German feminists today, for their part, have called for an exposé of how, in the nineteenth century, the labor movement split the women's movement" (12–13).

5. In a 1984 article entitled "Black Feminism in *For Colored Girls . . .*" by Ntozake Shange, I used the text presumed familiar to my German audience, *Shedding*, to illuminate the African American's work and found striking similarities:

> We find a number of common themes based mainly in gender and transcending differences in race. Among these . . . are: initiation— usually into heterosexuality, but in female separatist literature, into homosexuality as well; attitudes toward one's own body, its ugliness rather than its beauty; desire and lack of fulfillment, usually related to disappointed expectations in men; and the descent into madness, as both a hardship and a promise of new strength. . . . In *Haütungen,* the heroine's flirtation with insanity in the closing chapter is a deliberate attempt to assume the alienation assigned to women in phallocratic culture. Having experienced her body mainly as an engine for the male's will to dominate, and not as a generator of self-fulfillment, [the protagonist] retreats from society in order to cultivate a new awareness of her physical and mental make-up. Distancing herself from the environment, feeling menaced by the potential intrusion of others into this hermetic space, she slowly and painfully explores her courage to face the world again in [a] new skin. Whereas *Haütungen* ends on this note, *For Colored Girls . . .* is framed by [the theme of madness]. (185)

The difference, of course, lies in attitudes toward men, dispensable to the white author, necessary to the struggle for the black author.

6. A most thorough and succinct discussion of this point is Barbara Lawrence's essay "Four Letter Words Can Hurt You," which first appeared in the *New York Times,* 27 October 1973:

> The best known of the tabooed sexual verbs, for example, comes from the German *ficken,* meaning "to strike"; combined according to Partridge's etymological dictionary *Origins,* with the Latin sexual verb

futuere: associated in turn with the Latin *fustis,* "a staff or cudgel"; the Celtic *buc,* "a point, hence to pierce"; the Irish *bot,* "the male member"; the Latin *battuere,* "to beat"; the Gaelic *batair,* "a cudgeller"; the Early Irish *bualaim,* "I strike"; and so forth. It is one of what etymologists sometimes called "the sadistic group of words for the man's part in copulation." (376)

7. Similar also is the theme of language. Stefan explains the source of one linguistic innovation in the latter text: "Together with a lover I translated Wittig and Zweig into German. As the authors' wished, we worked from the English version, thereby introducing the idea of the 'companion lover,' *Liebesgefährtin,* into German. In [*Literally Dreaming*] I use *companion lover, Gefährtin,* instead of *lover, Geliebte* because the new term contains the roots "fahren" (to move/travel), "Gefahr" (danger), and implies "gefährlich" (dangerous)" (personal communication).

8. One major theoretical text, "required reading" for German feminists is Christina Thürmer-Rohr's *Vagabundinnen: Feministische Essays* (translated into English by Lise Weil). Also appearing in 1987, it is the embodiment of "pessimism" in that it urges us to "take leave of the principle of hope" and in these "murderous" times "attempt to live in the present without hope" (25; my translation).

9. Discussion/interview took place at Verena Stefan's home in Zöschingen, West Germany, 29 January 1989.

References

Altbach, Edith Hoshino. "The New German Women's Movement." In *German Feminism: Readings in Politics and Literature.* Edited by Edith Hoshino Altbach, Jeanette Clausen, Dagmar Schultz, and Naomi Stephan, 3–26. Albany: State University of New York Press, 1984.

Anders, Ann. "Fiktiver Brief an Verena Stefan." *Aesthetik und Kommunikation* 25 (September 1976): 120–21.

Bammer, Angelika. *Partial Visions: Feminism and Utopianism in the 1970s.* New York: Routledge, 1991.

Becker-Cantarino, Barbara. "Feministische Germanistik in Deutschland: Rückblick und sechs Thesen." In *Women in German Yearbook 8.* Edited by Jeanette Clausen and Sara Friedrichsmeyer, 219–34. Lincoln: University of Nebraska Press, 1993.

Bennett, Paula. "Critical Clitoridectomy: Female Sexual Imagery and Feminist Psychoanalytic Theory." *Signs* 18, no. 2 (Winter 1993): 235–59.

Bovenschen, Silvia. "Is There a Feminine Aesthetic?" Translated by Beth Weckmueller. In *Feminist Aesthetics*. Edited by Gisela Ecker. Translated by Harriet Anderson, 23–50. Boston: Beacon Press, 1985.

Brinker-Gabler, Gisela. "Alterity-Marginality-Difference: On Inventing Places for Women." In *Women in German Yearbook 8*. Edited by Jeanette Clausen and Sara Friedrichsmeyer, 225–45. Lincoln: University of Nebraska Press, 1993.

Brot ♀ Rosen (Bread ♀ Roses). *Frauenhandbuch Nr. 1*. Berlin: Verlag Frauen im Gerhard Verlag, 1974.

Brug, Gudrun, and Saskia Hoffmann-Steltzer. "Fragen an Verena Stefan." *alternative* 108–9 (June–August 1976).

Brügmann, Margret. *Amazonen der Literatur. Studien zur deutschsprachigen Frauenliteratur der 70er Jahre*. Amsterdam: Rodopi, 1986.

Caute, David. *The Illusion*. New York: Harper Colophon, 1971.

Cixous, Hélène. *la jeune née*. Paris: 10/18, 1975.

Clausen, Jeanette. "Our Language, Our Selves: Verena Stefan's Critique of Patriarchal Language." In *Beyond the Eternal Feminine: Critical Essays on Women and German Literature*. Edited by Susan L. Cocalis and Kay Goodman, 381–400. Stuttgart: Heinz, 1982.

———. "Verena Stefan." In *Women Writers in German-Speaking Countries*. Edited by Elke Frederiksen and Elizabeth Ametsbichler. Westport, Conn.: Greenwood Press, 1994.

de Lauretis, Teresa. "Feminist Studies / Critical Studies: Issues, Terms, and Contexts." In *Feminist Studies / Critical Studies*. Edited by Teresa de Lauretis, 1–19. Bloomington: Indiana University Press, 1986.

Eichmann-Leutenegger, Beatrice. "Eine verspätete Kunde vom natürlichen Leben" (Tardy News of Natural Living). Review of *Wortgetreu ich träume. Vidwalder Volksblatt*, 23 January 1988. Arche Verlag Archives.

Faderman, Lillian. *Odd Girls and Twilight Lovers: A History of Lesbian Life in Twentieth-Century America*. New York: Penguin, 1991.

Faludi, Susan. *Backlash: The Undeclared War against American Women*. New York: Crown, 1991.

French, Marilyn. *The War against Women*. New York: Summit, 1992.

Frieden, Sandra. "Shadowing/Surfacing/Shedding: Contemporary German Writers in Search of a Female *Bildungsroman*." In *The Voyage In: Fictions of Female Development*. Edited by Elizabeth Abel, Marianne Hirsch, and Elizabeth Langland, 304–16. Hanover: University Press of New England, 1983.

Goettle, Gabriele. "Brief der Schwarzen Botin an die Teilnehmerinnen des Münchner Frauenkongresses" (Letter from the Black Messenger to

Participants of the Munich Women's Congress). *Die Schwarze Botin,* no. 3 (April 1977): 5.

Grossman, Atina, and Sara Lennox. "The Shadow of the Past." Review of *German Feminism: Readings in Politics and Literature,* edited by Edith Hoshino Altbach, Jeanette Clausen, Dagmar Schultz, and Naomi Stephan. *Women's Review of Books* 4, no. 12 (1987): 15.

Joeres, Ruth-Ellen B. " 'Language Is Also a Place of Struggle': The Language of Feminism and the Language of American *Germanistik.*" In *Women in German Yearbook 8.* Edited by Jeanette Clausen and Sara Friedrichsmeyer, 247–57. Lincoln: University of Nebraska Press, 1993.

K.L. "Stadt/Land/Fluß . . ." (City/Country/River). *Prima Donna / Berliner Frauenzeitung,* no. 13 (February–March 1988). Arche Verlag Archives.

Lawrence, Barbara. "Four Letter Words Can Hurt You." In *Patterns of Exposition 10.* Edited by Randall E. Decker, 375–79. Boston: Little, Brown, 1986.

Levin, Tobe Joyce. *Ideology and Aesthetics in Neo-Feminist German Fiction: Verena Stefan, Elfriede Jelinek, Margot Schroeder.* Ph.D. diss., Cornell University, 1979.

Levin, Tobe, and Gwendolyn Flowers. "Black Feminism in *For Colored Girls Who Have Considered Suicide When the Rainbow Is Enuf.*" In *History and Tradition in Afro-American Culture.* Edited by Günter H. Lenz, 181–93. Frankfurt am Main: Campus, 1984.

Marti, Madeleine. *Hinterlegte Botschaften: Die Darstellung lesbischer Frauen in der deutschsprachigen Literatur seit 1945.* Stuttgart: Metzlar, 1992.

Mosler, Kathrin. "Der Mensch meines Lebens bin Ich. Uber 'Haütungen' von Verena Stefan" (The Person in My Life Is Me). *Frauenoffensive Journal 5* (1976): 51.

Muller, Johanna. "Ich bin meine eigene Muse" (I Am My Own Muse). *Norddeutscher Rundfunk,* 10 September 1977 (from the publisher's files).

Praesent, Angela. "Gute Winde sind weiblich, schlimme männlich" (Good Winds Are Female, Bad Are Male). Review of *Wortgetreu ich träume. Die Weltwoche,* 21 January 1988. Arche Verlag Archives.

Pulver, Elsbeth. "In der Grundform ankommen: Zu einem neuen Buch von Verena Stefan" ("Arriving at the Basic Form of the Verb: On a New Book by V. S."). *Neue Zuricher Zeitung,* 5 February 1988. Arche Verlag Archives.

Rich, Adrienne. *Of Woman Born: Motherhood as Experience and Institution.* New York: W. W. Norton, 1976.

———. *Der Traum einer gemeinsamen Sprache.* Translated by Gabriele Meixner and Verena Stefan. Munich: Frauenoffensive, 1982.

Schlaeger, Hilke. "The West German Women's Movement." *new german critique* 13 (special feminist issue) (Winter 1978): 59–68.

Schmidt, Ricarda. *Westdeutsche Frauenliteratur in den 70er Jahren*. Frankfurt: Fischer, 1982.

Stefan, Verena. "Foreword to *Shedding*" Translated by Johanna Moore and Beth Weckmueller. In *German Feminism: Readings in Politics and Literature*. Edited by Edith Hoshino Altbach, Jeanette Clausen, Dagmar Schultz, and Naomi Stephan, 53–54. Albany: State University of New York Press, 1984.

———. *Es ist Reich gewesen*. Frankfurt am Main: Fischer, 1994.

———. *Mit Füssen mit Flügeln*. Munich: Frauenoffensive, 1980.

———. *Shedding*. Translated by Johanna Moore and Beth Weckmueller. New York: Daughters, 1978. Originally published as *Häutungen*. Munich: Frauenoffensive, 1975.

———. *Wortgetreu ich träume*. Zurich: Arche, 1987.

Thürmer-Rohr, Christina. *Vagabundinnen: Feministische Essays*. Berlin: Orlanda, 1987.

Watkins, Renée. Personal communication, 28 February 1989.

Wittig, Monique, and Sande Zweig. *Lesbische Völker. Ein Wörterbuch*. Translated by Gabriele Meixner and Verena Stefan. Munich: Frauenoffensive, 1983.

The Feminist Press at the City University of New York offers alternatives in education and in literature. Founded in 1970, this nonprofit, tax-exempt educational and publishing organization works to eliminate stereotypes in books and schools and to provide literature with a broad vision of human potential. The publishing program includes reprints of important works by women, feminist biographies of women, multicultural anthologies, a cross-cultural memoir series, and nonsexist children's books. Curricular materials, bibliographies, directories, and a quarterly journal provide information and support for students and teachers of women's studies. Through publications and projects, The Feminist Press contributes to the rediscovery of the history and the emergence of a more humane society.

New and Forthcoming Books

The Answer/La Respuesta (Including a Selection of Poems), by Sor Juana Inés de la Cruz. Critical edition and translation by Electa Arenal and Amanda Powell. $12.95 paper, $35.00 cloth.

Australia for Women: Travel and Culture, edited by Susan Hawthorne and Renate Klein. $17.95 paper.

The Castle of Pictures and Other Stories: A Grandmother's Tales, Volume One, by George Sand. Edited and translated by Holly Erskine Hirko. Illustrated by Mary Warshaw. $9.95 paper, $19.95 cloth.

Challenging Racism and Sexism: Alternatives to Genetic Explanations (Genes & Gender VII), edited by Ethel Tobach and Betty Rosoff. $14.95 paper, $35.00 cloth.

Folly, a novel by Maureen Brady. Afterword by Bonnie Zimmerman. $12.95 paper, $35.00 cloth.

Japanese Women: New Feminist Perspectives on the Past, Present, and Future, edited by Kumiko Fujimura-Fanselow and Atsuko Kameda. $15.95 paper, $35.00 cloth.

The Slate of Life: More Contemporary Stories by Women Writers of India, edited by Kali for Women. Introduction by Chandra Talpade Mohanty and Satya P. Mohanty. $12.95 paper, $35.00 cloth.

Songs My Mother Taught Me: Stories, Plays, and Memoir, by Wakako Yamauchi. Edited and with an introduction by Garrett Hongo. Afterword by Valerie Miner. $14.95 paper, $35.00 cloth.

Women of Color and the Multicultural Curriculum: Transforming the College Classroom, edited by Liza Fiol-Matta and Mariam K. Chamberlain. $18.95 paper, $35.00 cloth.

Prices subject to change. *Individuals:* Send check or money order (in U.S. dollars drawn on a U.S. bank) to The Feminist Press at The City University of New York, 311 East 94th Street, New York, NY 10128-5684. Please include $3.00 postage/handling for one book, $.75 for each additional book. For VISA/MasterCard orders call (212) 360-5790. *Bookstores, libraries, wholesalers:* Feminist Press titles are distributed to the trade by Consortium Book Sales & Distribution, (800) 283-3572.